THE CHAMPION WITHIN YOU

How to Overcome Problems, Obstacles
and Adversity in Your Life

THE CHAMPION WITHIN YOU

How to Overcome Problems, Obstacles and Adversity in Your Life

To Ed & Jane,
Best wishes
Stan Frager

Dr. Stanley R. Frager

Champion Press

Many people have helped in the preparation of this book. I particularly want to thank the following:

Cheryl Cole, M.A., Star Lewis, Mark Reese, Ed Rosenbluh, Ph.D., Julie Segal, M.Ed., Stuart A. Tross, M.A., Gary Zachariah, M.A., Rich Wilkins, Neil Sexton, Lorena Peters and Janet Rockafellar. From the University of Louisville: Sandy Garcia and Cathy Horsman.

Cover and Jacket design by Barry Brawner, back cover photo by Herman Wyssbrod.

And thanks especially to my children, Sarah and Joshua, who keep me going when things get the roughest.

First Printing 1992
Second Printing 1993
Third Printing 1994
Fourth Printing 1998

A Letter to You

To: A Possible Friend

They would say, "Gee, Frager, you have heart, you're a courageous man." I have never thought of the events in my life as tests of courage. Specifically, I refer to one event: being diagnosed with colon cancer 16 years ago. As I will explain, it was not a matter of being a hero, but rather a matter of putting my life and its destiny in a proper perspective.

I had been having symptoms for almost a year before I actually went to see a physician to find out what was happening to my body. Even though deep down I felt that I was probably ill, I rationalized by giving myself a very minor, ordinary diagnosis. It was only because of my father's love and perseverance that I finally ended the procrastination and went to see a physician.

My father and I were on our first trip together in a very long time. Due to our careers, we often went far too long without spending quality time together. This vacation was time together to be cherished. During the course of the trip, however, my dad saw visible signs that I was physically ill. After we returned home, my father called me long distance every single night to inquire whether I had gone to see a doctor. Both of my parents pursued the issue with endless determination. I finally agreed after three weeks to see a doctor. I jokingly told my parents it was because I felt guilty that they were running up such an expensive long distance bill.

I had no idea how the events following the appointment would so profoundly affect the rest of my life. My family physician immediately sent me to a surgeon's office, where extensive tests were run. Dr. Watterman came in the room when the tests were completed, glanced at the chart, and matter-of-factly said, "It's cancer, and we need to operate as soon as possible." Because of my commitment as assistant coach for the University of Louisville baseball team, I wanted to be at their games the following week. So I scheduled my surgery for seven days from my initial appointment with the surgeon. I survived the surgery, but was given a daily reminder of my bout with cancer — a permanent colostomy. The real issue, however, was not surviving the surgery, but the possible threat of a recurrence that might lie ahead.

Thus, after the surgery I was forced to examine the situation constantly.

I chose to handle this adversity as I had others in my life. After all, this was really no different, only a little worse. I knew I had to do whatever I had to do to solve the problem. I underwent an extensive course of cobalt radiation treatment at the recommendation of a physician friend of mine who was a pioneer in radiation treatment, and coincidentally was the drummer in a band I had led during my collegiate years.

I truly felt that through my parents' love and persistence, my radiologist friend's advice, a fine surgeon, and the Lord above, my life had been saved. Thanks Al, Rose, Sam, Norton and my guardian from above.

I recently found out that studies have conclusively shown that surgery in adjunct with chemotherapy and/or radiation therapy greatly increases a patient's survival rate. I also learned that the mortality rate from the type and extent of colon cancer that I was diagnosed as having was about 90% the first year. Even though I didn't have that knowledge then, I never doubted that I would survive. I wanted to have a wife and children, and at age 35 I wasn't ready to admit defeat.

Sixteen years later, I now have those children. I am no longer married, a devastation worse than the diagnosis of cancer. My father is now deceased, a loss that cannot possibly be described. Still, people say, "Gee, Frager, you have heart and courage," but I continue to reply, "I am no martyr; like everyone else I merely do what I have to do."

This book contains my story and others' stories of overcoming adversity by simply "doing what they had to do," along with exercises to help you gain the skills of a CHAMPION . . . one who is able to overcome and conquer adversity.

Cordially,

Stan

FOREWORD

I look down with a strange, detached interest upon the impressive stack of papers which comprise my resume.

The list of accomplishments reads like a page from *Who's Who*. My educational background includes a Ph.D. and several pages of Continuing Education credits; seminars and workshops. From all appearances, it looks like this person has a pretty secure handle on his life.

I'm pretty diverse, too, I notice. I've won awards for film producing and directing. It says here that I'm a talented musician and dedicated scoutmaster; a noted educator and psychologist.

It occurs to me that this neat synopsis of my life would make a respectable obituary — a man's entire life reduced to paper. The memory will be nothing but a list of accomplishments. And when I'm gone, who will be left to be impressed?

My eyes scan the list: more appointments, more honors, associations, awards, and kudos, speeches, seminars. I've certainly been busy.

But where is the most recent part about the doctor telling me that the diagnosis is cancer, and the prognosis is grim? Where do these papers describe the invading cells that have ravaged my intestines and are continuing their destructive march through my body? First surgery, then radiation therapy. The mortality rate for this type of cancer is very high.

And if I do survive, what quality of life can I expect? I will spend the rest of my life toting around a plastic bag which will collect the wastes carried from my body by rerouting it into the opening carved into my abdomen.

Where is the part where the anger and the pain and the fear explode in a plaintive cry, "Why me?"

I mourn the wife I have not yet met. I mourn the children I will never have. These meaningless sheets of paper are mere words and I would put a match to them in an instant if it would mean a chance to live and to love beyond my 36th year.

That was sixteen years ago. Somewhere along the way I stopped asking "Why me?" and began to understand "Why not me?" For if there is one constant in this life, it is *adversity*. To varying degrees, we all encounter it at some point. Most of us are quite skilled in handling it in small doses. Accepting adversity is one of the conditions of being a citizen of planet Earth.

I was no stranger to adversity. I had been through four motorcycle accidents before wisely retiring my helmet. I had narrowly escaped death when I developed a thrombo called phlebitis (as a result of one of the accidents), which led to a pulmonary embolism. Adversity had also taken the form of job stress and pressure many times in my life.

I slowly came to realize that this new adversity, this particularly malignant form of cancer, was no different—just worse. The very skills I had used to overcome earlier adversity were the skills I now needed to summon to meet this deadly challenge.

I chose not to focus on the high mortality rate of this form of colon cancer. I chose to focus on the survival rate. I learned to concentrate on what I could have, not what I wouldn't have.

I have two beautiful children from a beautiful marriage. Although I shall always have my children, it is not so for my marriage. But it is a chapter in my life that would never have been written had I simply accepted the fate of my cancer and quietly gone off to wherever it is that we go. It is a chapter that I shall cherish, and I will go on to write new chapters for the life I reclaimed for myself thirteen years ago.

Just when you think you have conquered your final challenge, slain your last dragon, and you are awaiting the expected spoils of victory that you so richly deserve, life has a way of reminding you that you're not done yet.

Having gone through what I did with the cancer, surgery, radiation therapy, and recovery, I thought I had swallowed my ration of adversity. Living with a colostomy is a daily reminder of my pain and my victory, as well as a reminder of my continuing challenge. But it did not prepare me for the pain of hearing a little voice cry out, "Daddy, don't leave me."

So, I am writing this book for myself. I am also writing this book for the millions who have successfully surmounted far bigger obstacles than I, and who bear burdens far heavier than mine.

I write this for you.

CONTENTS

Chapter One

THE MEANING OF "SUCCESS"

*Success is measured not so much by the position that
one has reached in life as by the obstacles which he has
overcome while trying to succeed.*

Booker T. Washington

There have been literally thousands of books written on "success"...that elusive grade of excellence that defies quantification. Science has not yet discovered the yardstick that can accurately measure success. There are no gauges, no calipers, no scales with which we may determine the presence or absence of success. The thousands of books, treatises, and articles that have attempted to do this have arrived at only one common formula: The number of definitions of success is equal to the number of persons defining it.

Were there but one gene, one chromosome that programs humans to succeed, or advance toward success, scientists could set about the business of researching, dissecting and analyzing it. It would be a scientific breakthrough of huge proportions, and this newly discovered factor would undoubtedly bear the name of its discoverer. Fragerium has a nice ring to it.

Unfortunately, science has not isolated such an element, nor do I purport to have the answer. Despite the lack of concrete proof and precise definition of success, we do engage in its pursuit with fervor.

But without knowing what it is, how can we achieve it? It is much like suggesting to an Australian bushman that he can fly an airplane. Without even knowing what an airplane is, he is most severely handicapped, and yet has seen them fly overhead many times.

The scientific process often has to deal with such gray areas. What scientists do then is examine the evidence. Conclusions are subsequently based upon the evidence that we are able to extrapolate.

We accept the existence of glaciers on the strength of the evidence they left behind. The gorges and the canyons, the striations, the lakes—all physical documentation through which we conclude an Ice Age crept over our continent.

May we define success then as a sum total of its parts . . . only some parts of which are evident, observable, and measurable?

These parts can give us clues to the nature of this whole we call success. Just as paleontologists use the clues provided by fossils to deduce the condition of our planet millions of years ago, we can use behavioral clues to deduce the nature of the human condition we call success.

This, then, is not to be another attempt at defining the indefinable. Instead, we will look at the clues and the evidence provided by those people commonly judged as successful. And we will narrow the scope to an investigation of one facet of a successful person — *the ability to triumph over adversity*. We will focus on common qualities shared by those who exhibit a strong ability to overcome adversity.

We routinely assume that specific qualities are shared by people who share a specific talent. For example, research has shown that talented singers have a larger lung capacity than the average person. Those with artistic ability share *right-brain dominance*. Martial arts experts share the ability to focus precisely their energies at will. Consequently, it is reasonable to assume that those with the ability to overcome adversity also share one or more common qualities.

What, then, are these common qualities? Are they innate or acquired? What is it within one person—that is absent in another—that permits him or her to surmount an obstacle?

It is my hope that by identifying these qualities, we can provide an "inventory" of the necessary parts from which others may draw. It is my wish that the qualities we identify will be a schematic for triumph.

Chapter Two

GOING AGAINST THE CURRENT

*The greatest thing in this world is not so much where we
are, but in what direction we are moving.*
                                        Oliver Wendell Holmes

What is adversity? The word itself stems from the Latin adjective *adversus*,
which means "opposite," or "in the opposite direction." *Adverso fiumine* is a Latin
phrase meaning "upstream." What a vivid picture this paints for us! Upstream.
Going against the current. Have you ever tried to paddle a canoe upstream? It
is difficult even for the very strong. For others, it is an exercise in frustration.
For each stroke of the paddle blade, you fall behind half a canoe length, so you
must paddle very hard just to maintain your position. If you rest for even a
moment, the current will draw you downstream swiftly and surely. Many decide
that the destination upstream isn't worth the effort, and they choose to float back
downstream, letting the river chart their course. It is easier, and it is comfortable.
Adversity, then, is like an opposing force. It is anything that sets itself in the way
of our goals and works against us.

Consequently, the definition of adversity is largely dependent upon what
your goals are and where your priorities lie. One person's adversity may be
another's annoyance. For example, for a farmer whose livelihood is tied up in his
harvest, a severe drought is a devastating setback. It threatens his home, family,
and perhaps even his self-image. However, to a suburbanite hooked into city
water, the drought means merely annoying lawn-watering ordinances and a
slightly higher grocery bill in the fall.

Of course, some perceptions of adversity are more universal than others.
Most people would classify blindness as a major adversity. If one of your goals
is to have a successful marriage and to have a large happy family, the discovery

that you carry the gene which determines Cystic Fibrosis is a major roadblock to your planned future. If one of your priorities in life is to live lavishly and in comfort, a business failing is a decided setback.

So, it is important to understand that one's perception of adversity is colored by what we want, what we value or, as Oliver Wendell Holmes said, "What direction we are moving in." For some, the goal is as basic as survival: "I want to live." For others it is more complex: "I want to live and I want to live in such and such a manner." Or, even more complex still: "I want to live, and I want to live in such and such a manner, and I want to accomplish x, y, and z in the process." The more complex the goals, the more likely we are to be touched by adversity.

When I was diagnosed as having cancer, my immediate goal was survival. The triumph over death was my upstream battle. But more than just wanting to live, I wanted to live the kind of life I had envisioned for myself before I had the cancer. I wanted a wife and children. And then, beyond that goal lay the desire to accomplish so much more in my profession. I wanted to write, to speak, to have my own company. Again, move the destination further upstream. And with each added mile I needed to paddle came stronger currents, fallen trees, and hidden, jagged rocks. The relationship of adversity to the complexity of goals is exponential. In plain English, the more you want, the harder it is to get.

Consequently, it is no accident that people who have aspired to greatness seem to have a longer list of obstacles they have met in life. It is a natural pattern. If you choose to paddle but one stream during your life, you would have but one current to challenge you. But in paddling many streams, each one would present you with a new current unlike the last.

There is great hope to those of us who aspire to many streams in life. For with each upstream journey we learn something about that river, and about ourselves and our own abilities. We learn our strengths and our weaknesses, the power and strength of the current, and how to negotiate that river to maximize our strength and to shield our weaknesses.

For some, adversity makes its first appearance at birth in the form of a congenital disease or deformity. For others, life is much kinder for a time. And I say "for a time" because adversity does come to each of us at some point in our lives. All destinations cannot lie downstream. At some point in our lives we will need to stop drifting with the current, pick up that paddle, and work our hardest.

What is the alternative? If you don't start paddling for all you're worth, you will inevitably be carried downstream. For some, this is the course of choice, and they are entitled to it.

Just ahead, we will examine the stories of men and women who chose to pick up their paddles. They chose to forego the easy, sometimes peaceful ride on the current. Some of them have told their stories publicly in the media. Others are not celebrities in the Hollywood sense of the word, but are people just like you and me. They could be your next-door neighbor. One thing I have discovered in my years of clinical practice is that everyone has a story.

Some of the people we will be looking at are not successes in the dramatic, stellar sort of way that inspires movie scripts or sensational best-sellers. They are successes because they have survived. They met adversity and they accepted the challenge. They paddled upstream longer and harder than they ever dreamed possible. For some, the upstream journey was a continual battle against the forces of adversity, a river with no source, no final landing, no resting place. For others, the upstream journey was a temporarily charted course, and the expedition was a success.

As we follow their journeys we must look at their patterns, so that when it comes time for our journey, and we think we cannot paddle one more bone-wearying mile, we can pick up that pattern and cloak ourselves in its threads.

By identifying the common qualities in people who have overcome their adversities, we gather the pictures needed to visualize our own upstream journey. In my counseling practice I have learned the great power of visualization. YOU MUST SEE YOURSELF DOING WHAT YOU MUST DO. I have worked with hundreds of people in my practice to assist them in visualizing these things for themselves.

Athletes have long known the power of visualization. Jack Nicklaus SEES himself sinking the putt before he addresses the ball. Former University of Louisville basketball star Darrell Griffith SEES the ball swishing through the net before he shoots. Diver Greg Louganis SEES the perfect pike, the silent, clean slice of his body through the water.

Visualization is a skill we can acquire. For some, the skill is more easily learned. Others must struggle to see the picture. But by identifying the composite parts of the picture titled "Overcoming Adversity," we can more easily snip, clip, edit and splice the film to be played out in our heads. By being conscious of the kinds of human qualities shared by those who have met their opposing forces we need not feel helpless and unprepared when faced with ours. We will know which paddle to take along on our journey upstream. We will know the bow from the stern, and which strokes will steer us to port and which will steer us to starboard. We will have great hope and encouragement in knowing that there are millions of people who have gone before us and conquered their rivers.

My hope is that you will see something of yourself in this book. My belief is that you will. For by simply picking up this book and reading this far, you are saying that you will not be simply carried downstream by whatever currents life may bring. Use the navigational aids of the following conquerors who have charted their courses up the river. Use their experience to help map your course, and to reinforce your innate skills and strengths to move upstream.

Chapter Three

CHAMPIONS

A man of character finds special attractiveness in diffi-
culty, since it is only by coming to grips with difficulty that
he can realize his potential.

Charles DeGaulle

Continually referring to "those who have overcome adversity" is awkward and impersonal; plus, it's a mouthful. So I thought long and hard for the right word to capture their essence.

"Winners" sounded good until I thought about its implications. It implies the opposite — "losers." That is too negative, an indictment I do not wish to make of people who may not be as visibly successful in overcoming adversity. For the same reason, I discarded "achiever."

Eventually, I decided on Champion. Being a Champion does not imply that others are losers. It is not a word heavily loaded with absolutes or negative connotations. It does not have a true opposite. In our society, a Champion is someone who reaches for the stars, and often comes away with a handful, but not always. It is the reaching that makes a Champion.

Within each Champion you will find some measure of the following qualities:

Confidence
Heart
Adaptability
Motivation
Perspective
Initiative
Optimism
Network of Support

Each of the letters in the word Champions is a component of the whole word. Similarly, each of the qualities is a part of the whole person — the Champion. They interrelate. They feed and nurture each other with different intensities, providing a kaleidoscope of variations until the right combination comes together. Each person, as a unique individual with varying strengths and weaknesses, finds his own combination to become a Champion.

Please look carefully at each of these qualities and personal resources, for in them you can discover your own strengths — strengths which you can draw upon now, and strengths which you can build upon. You will also discover weaknesses which you will want to turn into strengths, because those are your vulnerable areas.

Each of these qualities has several components of its own. For example, the quality of confidence is made up of self-image, self-reliance, certainty, and sense of control. Everyone has some measure of strength in even just one of these areas. No one is completely void of personal resources. This is extremely encouraging to those of us who feel less than capable of coping with adversity.

You will find that you already possess many of the qualities of a Champion, perhaps more than some of the people we will be discussing. For none of these people I have talked with felt *totally* adequate to handle the adversity or obstacles in life.

In examining specific cases of individuals who have successfully and dramatically overcome adversity, it becomes fairly evident that there is a common ground shared by these people. While individuals have coping mechanisms peculiar to themselves, there are still several qualities of character that emerge over and over again. These qualities seem to appear, albeit in different forms, without regard to background, experience, genetics, or environment.

In many cases, these common qualities made their first appearance during the course of a personal trial. It was a quality the individual was unaware of. Have you ever found yourself reading a particularly heroic story in the newspaper and then thinking, "I could never do that"? Chances are, the hero of the story would have said the same thing until actually faced with the challenge.

We often limit ourselves by our own mental processes. We cannot see ourselves in situations so we cannot see the behavior needed to cope with them.

A thirty-eight year old mother of three children once told me, "People say what a saint I am. That's so far from the truth. If I had been up on that altar on my wedding day and the priest had said to me, 'Do you promise to love, honor, and cherish your husband; oh, and three children who have cerebral palsy and are profoundly retarded?' I would have said 'I don't, I won't, and I can't.' And I would have run for my life. It's just not something you plan on doing."

The people who share their stories in this book and thousands of others are not doing so merely for your entertainment. Nor are they doing it for a round of applause. They are telling their stories in the belief that we can all learn from each other, and we can gain valuable insight about ourselves in the process.

The qualities shared by these overcomers are not intended as an exhibit for you to walk by. We cannot simply add them up, nod our heads, and cluck knowingly, "Yup, he's got what it takes. No wonder he made it!" We are then simply thermometers, measuring the heat of the passion and human spirit which drive them. Could it be that the qualities found in the overcomers are instead thermostats which determine the level of passion and human spirit? And if so, does it not follow that by cultivating these qualities we can set our own thermostats to that same level?

I look at it this way. Some athletes are born with genetically superior talents. Natural athletes, we call them. Babe Didrickson Zaharias was one. She set two world records in two separate events in track in the 1932 Olympics. She went on to distinguish herself in basketball and baseball. Then the sport of golf caught her fancy. Never having played the game before, Babe nonetheless went on to become the first lady of women's golf, paving the way for the modern Ladies Professional Golf Association.

She was as comfortable with a golf club as anyone. On the other hand, we have Calvin Peete. For the poor black boy from the south with the deformed arm, the rich, white man's sport seemed an unlikely choice. Golf did not come naturally to him.

But Calvin disregarded the fact that he did not have all the traditional makings of a successful golf pro. Instead, he watched the natural athletes until he *understood* the components of a good swing. Then he adapted them to fit his limitations and took them on as his own. Today, Calvin Peete is known as one of the steadiest, straightest hitters on the tour.

Which one would you label as a good golfer—Babe or Calvin? Both?

Exactly. They're both good golfers. They both have the qualities that a good golfer has. The only difference is that for one the qualities were inherent, and for the other, the qualities were acquired. The bottom line is the scorecard, and it can't tell the difference.

Likewise, the bank can't tell the difference between a $5 million net worth statement of an heiress and a $5 million net worth statement of a hard working entrepreneur.

Some magnificent pieces of music have been composed by people who cannot read music; it simply comes naturally to them. Are some of the world's greatest symphonies any less great because they have been labored over for decades? We do not suppose that only composers who play by ear are the only ones capable of writing symphonies.

Why, then, do we limit ourselves by supposing that only people born with special qualities can be successful or overcome adversity? Can we not observe and learn and try to understand, so that we too can take on these qualities as our own? I believe we can.

Were you born knowing how to talk? Or did you acquire that skill by listening and learning? Did you emerge from your mother's womb knowing how to talk your way out of a traffic ticket or talk your way into a job?

Do you think that your qualities of generosity are inborn? If you do, spend a few hours at a pre-school and you'll soon understand that generosity is largely an acquired characteristic. We must be taught to share our sandpails!

Many qualities are acquired, but that does not lessen their power. Patience is an acquired characteristic. When was the last time you saw a hungry baby patiently waiting for its bottle? I would wager that even Job's mother snapped to attention at feeding time.

Perhaps it is the notion of a genetic predisposition to success that makes us feel inadequate to handle problems or adversity. We assume that only people born with "the right stuff" are somehow destined to overcome any obstacle, while we mere mortals can only hope never to be tested. This would explain the almost universal feeling among those who have overcome adversity that they are not heroes at all. They buy into the perception that only certain people are born of a certain caliber, and by mimicking any of their qualities, they become charlatans that will soon be exposed for what they are.

I know the feeling. After successfully battling my cancer and learning to live with the daily reminder of its presence, I continually hear people comment on how remarkable I am. A real survivor. A winner with the right stuff. Their comments are generally postscripted with an "I-don't-know-how-you-do-it-I-know-I-never-could."

All this pretty much puts me right up there with Moses, Hercules, and Joan of Arc, which of course I know is a big lie. Knowing the "hero" intimately has a way of erasing the mystique. I keep waiting for the day when someone pulls back the curtain to expose me frantically pulling the levers. "Oh, it's only Stan Frager!" they will wail; And that's who it is — only Stan Frager, not some superhuman born with special powers.

I suggest that we spend some time consciously working to develop the qualities of a survivor so that we aren't wondering how well-equipped we are to handle a crisis.

We equip our homes with smoke alarms not because we know with certainty that there's going to be a fire. Nor do we refuse to install a smoke alarm on the premise that by being prepared, we invite a fire. We do so because we feel better, safer, more in control. And why do we feel that way? Because statistics show that smoke alarms save lives. So if research shows that there are certain common qualities among people who have overcome adversity, why would we not prepare ourselves by cultivating these qualities? Indeed, that is all people do when they try to learn from the pain, suffering, and tragedy of others. They are trying to make sense of something incomprehensible, to make bad turn good. We do this not for others, but for ourselves.

Chapter Four

CONFIDENCE

As is our confidence, so is our capacity.
William Hazlitt

Let us begin at the beginning.

In the beginning of every Champion we find confidence.

Confidence is defined *as belief in one's own abilities; assurance; someone or something to be trusted* (Webster's New World Dictionary, 1988).

Over and over, I have found that Champions exhibit that belief in their abilities. They share an assurance, a certainty in themselves, often without a real basis for that assurance. However, as Hazlitt states above, "As is our confidence, so is our capacity." Champions do not let it bother them if they are less experienced or less prepared for a challenge than their neighbor. The feeling of "I know I can do it" is sufficient for their purposes.

The quality of confidence is the cornerstone upon which the other qualities of a Champion are built, and if we are to become Champions, then we, as well, must begin at the beginning.

We can begin by looking at the factors that influence confidence.

Self-Esteem

A wise person once said, "Self-confidence, in itself, is of no value. It is useful only when you put it to work."

Self-esteem is positive self-image, and self-image is how we see ourselves. When we look at ourselves in a mirror or in the glass of our mind's eye, what is the reflection that we see?

Do you see a strong, happy person? Capable? Clever? Kind? Lovable and loving? Resourceful? Brave? Or do you see someone weak and unhappy? Dull? Frightened? Helpless?

Your self-image is what you see, good or bad, factual or fictitious. Regardless, the image is true — as you see it. And who should know better? After all, it is *your* image.

A positive self-image is a prerequisite to confidence. If you cannot see yourself as someone who can be trusted, then no one else will see you that way, either. You will have low expectations, of both yourself and those around you, working as a powerful undercurrent sabotaging your efforts to get upstream.

Frank Epperson was born with spina bifida, a congenital cleft of the spine caused by the failure of the two parts of the spine to fuse during growth. Consequently, he is paralyzed from the waist down and is confined to a wheelchair. Frank's self-image provides the confidence found in a Champion. "Sure, I'm in a wheelchair. But I'm strong and healthy and I can hear well and I can do just about anything I set my mind to. I don't expect to be treated differently," he says. "Other disabled people complain to me that people treat them differently, and then they use that as an excuse for not trying. But listen to them—they *expect* to be treated differently, so of course they will be."

Indeed, self-image can be a very accurate predictor of the success or failure of an effort to overcome an obstacle.

It doesn't take a Ph.D. to figure out that the person who says, "I've never been very strong. I can't stand pain," is more likely to hand over the microfilm to his captors than the one who says, "I can stand anything." Now, the one who says he can stand anything doesn't know this as a scientific fact. He's not been through a comprehensive battery of everything there is to endure. And yet, there is a certainty there, a self-image of a brave, heroic person. Even if this man has never been called upon to do anything braver than retrieving a cat from a tree, he sees himself as brave.

With whom would you entrust your microfilm?

"I've never been very good with children," says the applicant for the baby-sitter's job, but her references are excellent. "I don't know how I do it, but somehow I manage to take good care of them." If you are anything like I am, you will bid her a quick farewell and hire the energetic teenager who admits to no experience but "adores children. We really get along."

External support available to the mothers of intellectually disabled children is thought to be less responsible for helping the mothers cope than the degree of her own self-esteem. The mothers with a positive self-image were better copers than those with average or low self-image, even when the average-to-lows had a very strong support network—family, friends, agencies, domestic help, counseling. Even going it alone, those mothers with good self-images fared better.

Self-complexity tends to buffer the adverse impact of stress or tragedy. Our self-esteem (positive self-image) is enhanced by the many aspects of ourselves. We feel more confident because we have a wider memory of successes from which we can draw.

A man we'll call David confides in me his feelings following the loss of his job. "As an architect, my whole picture of myself was as an architect. So when I was fired my self-esteem was shot to hell. Then I realized that I really was a lot of other things, too. I was a darn good father, and a pretty decent designer. So I combined the two and started my own business making creative playground equipment. It's small and I barely get by, but boy, do I feel good about myself!"

These are powerful arguments in favor of developing our own positive self-image, and working on more than one as well.

Self-image, good or poor, is entirely a learned experience. As infants, our original concept of ourselves as the center of the universe is reinforced by happy smiling faces around us with cuddling and cooing, and food at our bidding, or it is eroded by inattention, coldness, or belittling. As a learned experience, self-image can be affected by new input and re-learned. We can rewrite the script by rewriting the title character. We do this through visualization.

The human system cannot tell the difference between an actual experience and an experience imagined vividly, emotionally, and in detail. This is precisely why I encourage the athletes with whom I work to practice visualization. I cannot overstress how potent this practice can be.

Frank Epperson, while pushing at the wheels of his racing chair, sees himself reaching the crest of the seemingly endless hill, and then accelerating to breakneck speed, riding on the gift of gravity.

However, physical motion is not the only thing we can visualize. We can visualize emotion as well.

We say, "I see what you mean," or "I can see it all now!" We do not necessarily mean we are seeing with our eyes. We are seeing with our minds and our hearts. This is the kind of visualization we must use with our emotions. It is as powerful — or more — as visualizing a physical activity.

You have proved this to yourself hundreds of times. Remember lying in bed, alone in the house, and hearing a suspicious noise? Your heart rate quickened, the adrenaline pumped, and your muscles tightened. You were probably holding your breath. Your emotions visualized danger and your body did not qualify the threat as imagined. To you at that moment, the danger was real.

Remember the feeling of delicious anticipation you had as a child waiting for Santa Claus or for your birthday party? You were actually experiencing the pleasure before it had even happened! So powerful are these images that we are often disappointed with the real thing. We have been so skillful in visualizing that reality has a tough act to follow.

So you can see, you're already much of an expert at the technique. The key is to use it not as a replacement for reality, but as a catalyst for reality.

Alexander Jourjine saw himself as a free man. Jourjine's self-confidence and self-reliance provided him with the Champion's resources to overcome oppression and a bleak future. Jourjine, on his own with no "underground" assistance, escaped from the U.S.S.R. in a 23-day trek. On foot through forbidding country, Jourjine's dangerous plan set him up against sentries, border patrols, radar, electrified fences, and the lethal forces of nature.

His story is marked by extraordinary courage born of a certainty and confidence that his plan would succeed. Knowing the consequences of failure, Jourjine could not afford anything less.

He had gone over his plan hundreds of times in his mind—he *saw* himself crossing the border to freedom.

I remember the first public speaking tour I was invited to attend. As a Winston Churchill fellow, the first stop of the tour was The World Conference on Youth Unrest in Tel Aviv, Israel. As I was preparing to speak in front of forty people on "The Residential Treatment of Delinquents," my heart was beating at a rapid pace, my forehead was dripping with sweat, my mouth was very dry, and my hands were so sweaty and shaky that I was afraid to take a drink of water because if I did that, water would surely spill all over my suit. Afterward, I became very angry with myself. It was a very embarrassing and humiliating feeling to have become so intimidated by speaking to strangers about a subject in which I was fluent. So, like the Champions discussed above, I too realized that the only way to overcome this adversity was through visualization, and that is exactly what I did. I began practicing my speech in front of a mirror in the hotel room. I would picture myself under pressure, and would visualize myself being a Champion giving a good talk and receiving the applause and praise from my audience. Since that embarrassing day in Israel, every time I prepare myself for a talk, I always practice in front of a mirror visualizing myself being a Champion, and giving the best speech that I am capable of giving.

Little did I know how important learning how to visualize feelings would come into play in my life, until my diagnosis of colon cancer. After my surgery I forced myself on a daily basis to visualize a complete recovery and positive prognosis. This enabled me to see myself after the surgery getting better and stronger on a daily basis. I believe that my ability to visualize a successful recovery was a key element in my body's restoration to normal functioning.

How can this skill be used to enhance self-image? Well, if your body's system cannot distinguish between real and synthetic experience, you can feed it imagery that reflects whatever self you want to project. A study done at the University of California School of Medicine in San Francisco by psychologist Paul Ekman was able to document the body's response to visualization. Ekman and his colleagues had their subjects perform facial expressions to emote six specific emotions. Researchers measured increased heart rate and lowered skin temperature in the subjects displaying "fear." Expressing anger with facial expression caused the heart rate and the skin temperature to rise. In short, the study provides quantitative evidence to support the notion that our bodies cannot tell the difference between synthetic and real emotion. We can *use* our bodies and our actions to control the way we feel!

If you have never felt courageous, it might be hard at first to imagine that emotion. But like anything we learn, mastery comes with practice. It took you a lifetime to feed yourself the perceptions that make up your current self-image, so change will not happen overnight. Fortunately, however, results will be evident remarkably soon.

Stress — A "Vitamin C" Deficiency

Lack of confidence can invite stress, and one characteristic of confidence is the absence of stress.

Our society is obsessed with conquering the dreaded "S" disease. Stress is a virulent enemy that attacks the central nervous system and weakens our immune defenses, both physical and emotional. It is highly contagious and can be spread through casual contact at work, school, and home.

Stress is big news and big business.

The cover story for the April 25, 1988, issue of *Newsweek* was "Stress On The Job." The story dealt with the increasing cost of stress to business and personal lives, a cost that some experts estimate as high as $150 billion per year—almost the size of the federal deficit.

Before I get too far, I need to explain the use of the word "stress." It is currently fashionable to use the word as a catch-all to describe jangled nerves, or at the least the feeling of pressure. In behavioral studies however, the word "stress" is less trivialized, and is used in connection with serious life changes and difficulties, including tragedy. So in my continual use of the word stress, please understand its scope. Stress can be caused by death, illness, divorce — or a whole series of minor hassles, ranging from traffic jams to paperwork.

In a report by the former U.S. Surgeon General C. Everett Koop, he estimates that two-thirds of all illnesses before the age of sixty-five are preventable. Combined with research showing that vulnerability to illness is increased with stress, the impact of our stress-prone society is enormous. Fully fourteen percent of all occupational disease claims made in workmen's compensation cases are stress-related. A 1984 research report suggests that the toll of stress is higher than the suffering it exacts. Other studies indicate that certain kinds of cancer may be related to emotional loss, repression, inward direction of anger, and vulnerability to emotional loss.

"Twenty five years ago, we had more intermittent stress," says Atlanta therapist Geneva Rowe in the aforementioned *Newsweek* article. "We had a chance to bounce back before we encountered another crisis. Today, we have chronic, unremitting stress!"

In a survey by advertising agency D'Arcy, Masius, Benton and Bowles, three quarters of Americans indicate that they have stress caused by their jobs.

The National Center for Health Statistics showed figures from a 1985 study of 40,000 workers which indicated more than half reported experiencing "moderate" to "a lot" of stress in their jobs.

Clearly, these figures show an alarming trend.

If our day-to-day existence is so fraught with hassle-stress, how can we expect to cope in a *real* crisis?

Consider the wisdom of essayist Samuel Johnson, which is as pertinent today as it was over 200 years ago when he wrote it. In his essay "Jack Whirler," he describes the malady of modern America with the eye of an '80s stress-seminar psychologist:

"Jack Whirler lives in perpetual fatigue without proportionate advantage, because he does not consider that no man can see all with his own eyes or do all with his own hands, that whoever is engaged in multiplicity of business must transact much by substitution and leave something to hazard, and that he who attempts to do all will waste his life in doing little."

Samuel Johnson knew what behavioral psychologists have spent lifetimes researching. The "perpetual fatigue" that Johnson speaks of is the result of what we popularly call "stress" or the "Yuppie flu."

Stress, however, is not the disease it is made out to be. Rather, it is a symptom — a symptom of a deficiency of confidence, Vitamin "C." If we only treat symptoms, we never really eradicate the cause of the disease. We don't cure coughing; we cure pneumonia. By the same token we don't cure stress; we build confidence. Actually, we can never really eliminate stress, but we can keep it in remission.

Stress is unavoidable, and we shouldn't attempt to avoid it totally. Even if it were possible, withdrawal from all exposure to demands for change would mean a life so bland as to be virtually worthless.

Locus of Control — Who's in Charge Here?

A study of race car drivers shows that they are most stressed during pit-stops, not while speeding around turns at 200 miles per hour. The key here is control. The driver has his or her fate in his own hands when he is behind the wheel of a race car. Despite the risks, he retains control. The anxiety and distress are marked by his *lack* of control in the pits, where precious seconds tick away while he can do nothing.

This feeling of some measure of control over life's events is also a predictor of life satisfaction in older adults. These older adults who say that they are satisfied with their lives tend to recall their lives as being, for the most part, under their control.

Jobs that carry a high degree of responsibility but little power or authority are the most stress-prone. Inner city high school teachers, miners, air traffic controllers, waitresses, and customer service workers are on the Top Ten list. Why? If you analyze these workers, you'll see that much of their days are spent dealing with things over which they have no measurable control, or they lack the authority to exert an influence over the problems that occur.

It is the sense of control that determines the amount of stress an event will have on us. So a waitress who cannot get orders out of the kitchen because of a slow front-line cooking staff can conceivably feel more stress than a pilot aboard a 747 whose passengers' lives he holds in his hands.

The caricature of the back-seat driver is a classic example of the stress that is generated by lack of control. Unable to steer the car and thus maintain control, the back-seat driver experiences a high degree of anxiety, even when he may know that the driver is very capable. Perhaps the key to overcoming one's fear of flying may be in becoming the pilot.

Control over events seems to heighten perceived stress, but this is neutralized by an increased ability to adjust. In other words, having control can put the pressure on, but it also gives us the ability to adjust, which soothes the anxieties we may have in a situation.

Rollin Braden tells how he survived an incredible ordeal with two huge Alaskan Brown bears. Mauled and gnawed upon until the bears left him for dead, Braden lived to hunt another day. His ordeal did not consume him with fear. Instead it taught him a truth about himself. "I got myself into a situation I shouldn't have," says Braden. "And that's the key thing I have learned from all this: no matter what, keep in control. This goes not only for hunting, but for everything else in your life."

When British hostage negotiator Terry Waite was kidnapped in Beirut in January 1987, Fiona Glass could not imagine the anguish Waite's wife had to endure. "Oh, his poor wife! I could never handle anything like that!" she said. And yet, that is precisely what she would have to do six months later when her husband, Charles, was abducted by Lebanese terrorists.

Fiona responded with the qualities of a Champion. "I tried to intellectualize the situation so it became a puzzle to solve," she says. "Then, instead of feeling like a passive victim, I could feel I was actually doing something positive."

After my cancer surgery there were choices to be made. I could lie in my hospital bed feeling sorry for myself, or I could take charge and begin planning my recovery with the doctors. That is exactly what I did. Control was taken by visualizing myself having a successful recovery. I took control of my recovery by choosing post-operative radiation therapy (which was experimental at the time), writing journal articles about my surgery experience and colostomy, and by making arrangements and plans to get back to my normal routine; seeing clients, teaching, and being an assistant coach for the University of Louisville baseball team. I became driven to overcome this life-threatening disease, and chose to take control, giving me the feeling that, regardless of the prognosis of my cancer, the success or non-success of my recovery was in my hands.

It is the Champion's ability to find ways to regain control that is the crux of his seemingly superhuman confidence. One of the ways he does this is by calling up memories of past successes.

In recalling past successes, the Champion may be using accomplishments directly reflecting the current challenge, such as the public speaker quelling his jitters with memories of a stunning speech he delivered to a rapt audience. The diver attempting a new dive recalls successfully completing similar dives, and the bankrupt executive starting over recalls his early "lean" years successfully working up from the mail room. "I did it before. I can do it again," they think — or, "If I got through that, then this can't be much harder."

Tenacity is very much dependent upon the memory of past successes, and a near-amnesia of past difficulties or failures. (I say "near amnesia" because the lessons of our shortcomings must be retained.) In a Champion, the memory of past failures is selectively myopic, and the memory of success clear and sharp.

This would explain the almost incomprehensible tenacity of Champions in picking themselves up and continuing on, confident that the next time will be the charm.

The pitiful résumé that follows is a classic example of someone with selective myopia regarding past failures and consequent ability to remain confident:

Failed in business in 1831. Defeated for legislature in 1832. Second failure in business in 1833. Suffered nervous breakdown in 1836. Defeated for Speaker of the House in 1838. Defeated for elector in 1840. Defeated for Congress in 1848. Defeated for Senate in 1855. Defeated for Vice President in 1856. Defeated for Senate in 1858. Fortunately, in 1860, the populace believed in the man who believed in himself, and elected Abraham Lincoln President of the United States.

This legendary "success" story illustrates the power of recalling past successes. Those around you will also focus on your successes and ignore your failures and weaknesses if that is the image you project.

"Whatever adversity you face, you don't give up," says former Texas governor John Connolly. "You start over."

Connolly speaks from personal experience. He has started over many times. Struck down by a bullet from the same gun that killed President John F. Kennedy, Connolly recovered and went on to serve in President Nixon's cabinet. His failed bid for the Republican presidential nomination in 1980 sent him back to Texas. Once more adversity tested him. He was forced into retirement from his law firm, but he got up, brushed himself off, ventured into real-estate. Again, the Texan was to be knocked off his horse. When oil prices collapsed to one-quarter of their value, the economy came crashing. With it went the venture capital, and Connolly spent the next five years trying to salvage what he could. Eventually, there was only the bottom, and Connolly filed personal bankruptcy. Connolly watched as his personal items were auctioned off in return for legal tender that, in some instances, ironically bore his signature as Secretary of the Treasury.

"Two or three years from now, we'll be back," he says. "I am going to be making money."

There is a certainty there, born of confidence. Connolly is buoyed by the memory of his past successes and the view that failures are merely temporary.

Studies from the University of Illinois show that the power of negative thinking is more powerful than positive thinking. The memory of past failings or past trauma can be a potent predictor of future events. The memory of the negative event becomes the thing uppermost in our mind, and consequently may be a self-fulfilling prophecy. The memory of past failures or unhappy experiences tends to linger on and do its damage throughout life with those who exhibit an external locus of control; that is, outside factors have the control, not me. Those who feel somewhat helpless to determine life's events are much more likely to nurse old wounds, thereby reinforcing the failure or unhappy experience. Recent or current adversity is not even needed to make such a person unhappy. The past is sufficient to keep him down-trodden and beaten.

Champions know this instinctively, and concentrate on good memories and past successes. This points to the importance of keeping those negative thoughts out of our minds. We cannot help but shape our lives to what occupies our minds most often, and research indicates that negatives are the quickest to assimilate. Test your memory on it yourself. How many separate instances in grade school can you name where the teacher or classmate praised you for a great job? Now, think about the times you were ridiculed or rebuked. Pretty powerful memories, those negatives.

Life will deal us a handful of negatives without our encouragement and assistance. So don't dwell on them when they occur, and don't conjure up any. Engaging in a little self-pity now and then will happen, but remember that the embellishments you ascribe to your suffering may come back to haunt you. You can work up a real dread about going to the dentist based on one bad experience with a root canal. Catastrophizing events can even cripple you emotionally. The newly divorced woman who dwells on the sub-human aspects of her ex-husband and the insufferable situations she endured with him may only be engaging in harmless, therapeutic husband-bashing — for now. She may, however, be imprinting such powerful negative views of marriage in her memory that re-marrying may be a very scary proposition. Better copers tend to mull over and rehash the situation far less than those who did not adjust well.

Champions focus on success, while those who do not cope well focus on failures. In fact, studies show that depressed individuals not only focus on their failure, they attach more significance to the remembered failures than to remembered successes. These individuals also show a tendency to evaluate personal feedback in a self-derogating manner. What a confidence drain!

We have all seen the self-effacing, unsure apologizer. "Oh, that deal I clinched? It was pretty big, but it's a drop in the bucket compared to all the ones I lost. I won't be able to clinch another deal like this in a million years. It was sheer luck."

If we concentrate on the memory of our past failures, we would never have an Abraham Lincoln, a Thomas Edison, or a Wilbur and Orville Wright. We would have virtually no scientific breakthroughs, no antibiotics, no space program. Major league baseball players with a .400 batting average would focus on the 6 out of 10 times at bat they failed.

"Learned helplessness" is the term psychologists use to describe the debilitating memory of past failures. The theory of learned helplessness was formulated by Martin E.P. Seligman as a result of his observations that animals could be taught to be helpless. As a young graduate student at the University of Pennsylvania, Seligman observed a strange phenomenon during an experiment with laboratory animals.

In this experiment, dogs were being taught to escape an electric shock by selecting the correct escape route. The theory was that the next time through, the dogs would head right for the escape route without having to go through trial and error, having learned from their past success. What happened, however, was that these dogs did *not* head for the correct exit. They didn't even try to escape. Instead, they just sat there.

What Seligman discovered was that these dogs had been part of an earlier experiment in which the shock could not be escaped. Seligman surmised that the memory of the past failure taught the dogs that escape was futile. The *expectation* of total lack of control caused the animals to voluntarily relinquish their control and give up. The expectation, in effect, caused the failure.

Seligman went on to develop his theory in relation to human behavior, and much the same results appeared. In the past twenty years, it has been refined and adapted by Seligman and a host of others to reflect the question of why a helpless response is not always given by humans in the face of a seemingly hopeless situation. The revised helplessness theory was born. In a nutshell, the revised theory took into consideration that people, unlike dogs, often ask "Why?" And the answer we give to that 'Why?' determines whether or not we feel helpless.

Seligman calls the answer to the why-is-this-happening question "explanatory style," and I will be discussing this more in the chapter on Optimism. For the moment, suffice it to say that the reasons we attribute to our failures are the key.

If we believe, like the dogs in the experiment, that we do not have any control over the situation, we see ourselves as helpless, and by seeing ourselves so, we become helpless. As you will recall from the experiment with the dogs, the fact that dogs could escape was immaterial.

Washington Post columnist William Raspberry points out the self-defeating process of negative expectations. "We don't work very hard at things that we assume are beyond our ability to master."

Learned helplessness is exactly what it sounds like: we teach ourselves that we are helpless. We teach ourselves to believe that we do not have control, and we do this by recalling past failures.

Like many victims of child abuse, Karen M's childhood sexual abuse by her father and brother is a classic example of learned helplessness. The memory of each abuse episode and the inability to escape taught Karen that it was futile to try.

But, because this helplessness is learned, it can be unlearned. As Karen discovered, through a gradual build-up of self-esteem and coping methods, options began to appear and she began to retrieve the control that she had relinquished to external forces. When this happened many of her problems began to disappear. Depression lessened, and tension eased.

Seligman's work with the learned helplessness theory confirms that depression dissipates when depressed individuals are taught how to exert greater control on their environments and lives.

We learn at a very young age how to exert control. We cry and we cause mother to feed us, cuddle us, play with us. The child remembers the successes he has had with crying; he does not remember the failures. Children are remarkable models for us in seeing the power of the memory of past successes. They remember the one time they were able to badger Dad into backing off a restriction, and pay no mind to the twenty times that their Herculean efforts to persuade him failed. Now that's confidence!

Motivational speaker and writer Earl Nightingale shares with salespeople "The Strongest Secret." This "secret" is that we literally become what we think about most of the time.

Now, Mr. Nightingale did not dream up this profound truth. This notion has been around since the time of the great philosophers, the Bible, and on down through history. What makes this such a strange secret is the fact that so few people really understand it. And yet, it is so simple. This, in a nutshell, is what visualization is all about. *We become what we think about.*

For this reason, it is important to focus our thoughts on what we *want* to be. To clutter the mind with negative thoughts — what we *don't want* to be — invites disaster. We run the risk of becoming what we keep telling ourselves not to be.

Bottom line: An obsession with a negative is as powerful as an obsession with a positive. So at the risk of obsessing you with negatives, I will keep this section as short as possible.

Have you ever had a radio jingle play over and over in your head? The more you think about it and tell yourself *not* to think about it, the more loud it becomes. Do you remember what happened when you were a kid and a classmate said, "Don't think about elephants"? Of course! Elephants were the only thing you *could* think about.

If you fill your mind with thoughts on what you *shouldn't* be doing, your tactics will have an opposite effect. Since what you spend most of your time thinking about determines who you are, you become exactly what you had determined *not* to be. The mind has nothing else to work on.

So it is no wonder that there seems to be an epidemic of religious preachers falling to the very temptations about which they preach. That's all they think about! Their obsession with evil or sin — even though they preach against it — determines who they are and what they do. If they concentrated on the absence of sin, they might do better for themselves and their congregations.

The key here is that your thoughts determine your self-image, and your self-image is who you are. If you dwell on your infirmities, you think of yourself as infirm, and you *are* infirm. Psychosomatic illness is no less debilitating than an illness caused by real disease.

So — quit thinking about negatives! *Replace* those thoughts with positives. This is important. It is not enough to say quit thinking about . . . (remember the elephant?). You must put a thought, concept or notion in the vacancy you have created.

In the section following you will find the first of nine sets of stories and exercises to help you get to know the Champion within you. Each of us has untapped attributes — inner strength — that, with practice, we can learn to use to overcome difficulties in our lives, whether they be large or small, temporary or permanent.

Find a quiet, private place to sit and do the exercises on Confidence. Take your time. Allow yourself to answer the questions honestly. There are no right or wrong answers and you won't be graded, so don't be afraid of making a mistake. The Champion within you is there waiting to be discovered.

CONFIDENCE

Something to Think About and Do

Everyone knew that Christopher Cox was going places. At twenty-five years of age, he had already compiled an impressive resume. An honor graduate of the University of Southern California and a Summa Cum Laude alumnus of the Harvard Law School and the Harvard School of Business, Chris had to organize his job offers in four separate three-ring binders. As editor of the Harvard Law Review, he had come to the attention of the nation's most prestigious law firms.

He had chosen to serve his clerk-of-court tenure under the Honorable Judge Choy in Hawaii. For a young man who had spent the first eighteen years of his life in the bone-chilling climate of Minnesota, the opportunity to work with the respected judge offered some pleasant side benefits. Hawaii was an ultimate paradise befitting Chris' perfectly charted course.

But then one day his life careened wildly off course. It was August of 1977, and Chris was living in Honolulu. It was his habit to take mini-vacations to neighboring islands on the weekends, since his schedule did not permit real vacations of any length. This time he had decided to visit the island of Molokai. He and his friend, Mike Cook, headed out at 5 a.m. to take advantage of the low excursion rates offered at that time.

They arrived on schedule and went to pick up their rental vehicle. Since the island is largely uninhabited, roads are primitive or often non-existent. The only way to properly traverse the island is in a four-wheel-drive vehicle. Consequently, they were scarce. Molokai Fish and Dive in the town of Kaunakakai was the only place that rented them, and they had only four. Chris and Mike were not one of the fortunate few to get a "normal" four-wheel-drive.

"We didn't luck out by getting a normal jeep," Chris said. "We got this oversized jeep weapons carrier. It was a big, huge thing with locking hubs. You had to get out of it and physically turn each of the hubs on each of the four wheels in order to turn it into a four-wheel-drive. It was really an arduous thing. It was so difficult to lumber around in this thing and to turn it that Mike and I took turns driving. The steering wheel was just too heavy."

Their destination was the rain forest in the middle of the island, where nestled away in its midst was a set of gorgeous waterfalls. They captured the beauty and the seclusion on film, then knowing the difficulty they had getting up into the rain forest, decided to head back down early.

The trail was extremely muddy, and they could only travel about five miles per hour. The high center of gravity made the jeep unstable, and the ride was uncomfortable and bouncy. Sharp turns on the downhill mud trail made the cumbersome vehicle even more difficult to maneuver. As they approached one treacherous corner, the left wheel hit a grassy berm. Rather than simply bouncing as it had done before, the jeep's center of gravity shifted, and it began to tip.

"It tipped very slowly. We sat there thinking, 'Hey, we're turning over,'" he recalled, laughing. "'Yup, we're turning over.'" It was as if they were watching themselves in some strange, surrealistic movie being run in slow motion.

"It wasn't like we just flipped over. It just turned over very, very slowly, and it ended up on top of me. It landed sort of on an angle, with the passenger falling out, and me being pinned underneath."

The front end of the back cab came to rest directly across Chris' back. His legs were drawn up in a grotesque fetal position with his thighs pinned behind his ears. His left cheek was plastered into the shattered windshield, his twisted body the only thing between the tons of crushing steel and the mud of the rain forest. He knew that the human body could not assume such a position.

"I was in great pain," Chris remembered vividly. "It's like if someone puts a great weight on your shoulders and it's too much for you to take and you can't stand it any more. You yell, 'Take it off!' And someone does. But in this case nothing happens, and you're just stuck there. There is nothing you can do."

Since there were only four four-wheel-drive vehicles on the entire island, and Chris was underneath one of them, the likelihood that help was coming soon was not promising. The area was uninhabited and difficult to reach. There was no one to lift the unbearable weight from his back.

Mike was unable to move the monstrous jeep off of his friend. He would have to go for help.

Chris lay there alone, trapped, and in intolerable pain. The weight of the jeep continued its steady pressure, a trash compactor of human flesh, grinding his face further into the fragments of the windshield. His eyes now studded with glass shards, Chris prayed for unconsciousness.

Incredibly, unconsciousness did not come. With each succeeding minute, everything Chris knew about pain was being challenged. To this young attorney's analytical mind, it defied logic that such unbearable agony could continue. And whether or not the next half hour or so was a conscious decision on his part or a panic response, he does not know. After all, he says, "Even a panicked squirrel will do whatever it takes to free himself."

For approximately thirty torturous minutes, Chris willed his face, shoulders, and arms to make small movements in the ground beneath him. Millimeter by millimeter, he slowly dug a trench with his own body which allowed him precious inches of space between the jeep and the ground. Once he had created this meager escape tunnel and the slight freedom of movement it provided, he used his hands to claw the ground and pull himself out inch by inch.

To this day, he is not quite certain how he was able to remove himself. He later learned that his back was broken, and his legs were paralyzed.

His body out from under the crushing weight of the jeep, Chris could go no farther. The pain was too great to continue. His head remained underneath the jeep, though no longer pinned between steel and broken glass. A partially collapsed metal support from the top of the jeep was all that separated the tons of metal from Chris' head as he lay helpless in the rain forest of Molokai.

Miraculously, in his search for help, Mike ran into a native Hawaiian couple, who were up in the rain forests picking maile, tropical flowers used in making leis. Even more miraculously, they had a CB radio. They radioed Kaunakakai for an ambulance. The agonizing wait was made longer by the narrow, muddy terrain, which forced the paramedics to back up the trail since there would be nowhere for them to turn around once they reached Chris.

After being strapped into the ambulance, Chris remembers the paramedics working on his eyes with tweezers. They removed his soft contact lenses and they were studded with glass. "This could have been your eyeball," they told him.

He recalls the strange thing he did next. "I asked for a mirror." Unbelievably, someone obliged. His initial reaction was that, should he live, he would be disfigured for life. The handsome, dark-eyed man with the engaging smile was unrecognizable. His thoughts centered on his face, head, and upper body, unaware of the massive amounts of damage done to the rest of his body. He did not know that he was paralyzed, nor that he had severed a quadricep muscle in his leg. Even without this knowledge, he felt that he was "pretty much history."

He was taken to Molokai General Hospital, where he was given morphine, and treated for shock. He remembers being surprised that he did not "go down for the count." He remembers having a conversation with the doctor.

"They were unable to diagnose me, and he explained that. They had no idea what was wrong with me except that I was really beat up, and they were going to send me to Oahu. They just strapped me into a stretcher and shipped me off. I did sleep then."

"I woke up in Oahu at Queens Hospital, which is the best hospital in Oahu. I was prepped for surgery, and apparently Mike had filled out the paperwork. My doctor, Lawrence Gordon, was not around at the time. I was being attended by a resident, who while he was going through the paperwork said, 'I see you're a lawyer.' I said yes, and he said that in that case there were a few things he needed to discuss with me.'"

Chris laughs as he remembers the conversation. "He pointed out that it was 3 A.M., that he had already done four surgeries that day, and well, it had been a pretty long day. Not to suggest that there were any problems, of course... 'you'll still get the same fine surgery. I just wanted you to know,' he said. He told me that he had to operate immediately or we'd have to wait two weeks for all the cuts to heal. The risk of infection from these wounds when they cut you open for surgery is very high. So he told me we either do it now, which was already marginal as far as the danger of infection, or in two weeks."

Chris seems amused at the scenario. "I asked him what the negative side of waiting two weeks would be. He told me that there was serious spinal cord damage with jagged bones that could sever the rest of my spinal column. There was a serious dislocation besides the fracture, and he said that my spinal column was a tangled mess of threads. It looked like a coat hanger. Any movement could be the end of it."

Chris recalls asking the doctor how long he had been up. Since 6 A.M. the previous morning was the reply. "I told him to get a good night's sleep and if that meant I was going to be a paraplegic, so be it. But I wasn't about to agree to surgery after that."

For Chris, it turned out to be the right decision. Dr. Gordon had then returned, and as the best orthopedic surgeon on the islands, Chris felt confident. He was assisted by the original resident, as well as by a neurosurgeon. "Whenever your wiring is exposed, it's good to have an electrician," Chris noted wryly.

In the meantime, however, great pains had to be taken to ensure total immobility. He was placed on a huge sheepskin which would minimize the risk of bedsores and permit the nurses to move him while keeping him motionless.

"I could be in three positions. Flat on my back with no pillow, or on one side or the other. And when I was on my side, I was really on my side. Every six hours they would just rotate me, like a barbecued pig on a spit. In order to move me they would have these enormous nurses, each about 200 pounds or so — and they would line up alongside of me and wrap me up like a Tootsie-Roll in the sheepskin. Then they would say 'One, two, three,' and they would just turn me on a perfect pole. They made sure that my axis was completely straight so that nothing would cut through my spinal cord. Evidently it worked."

During the two-week period in which Chris awaited his surgery, each hour and each day of uncertainty weighed heavily. Had he made the right decision? His other injuries began healing, and after a week, they were able to wash his hair, and the swelling in his face had begun to gradually subside. Still not recognizable to himself in a mirror, Chris remembered the glass studded contact lenses and was grateful for the reflection, however distorted and swollen. During this time, Chris discovered that he was paralyzed from the waist down.

"They stuck all sorts of things in the soles of my feet to get a response," Chris said in recalling the realization of his paralysis. "They had this thing that looks like a pizza cutter with jagged edges. They would roll it up and down the soles of my feet and I couldn't feel a thing."

There was no reaction to the reflex testing either. The little hammer tapping on Chris' knee did not elicit the normal kick reflex. His legs lay motionless on the sheepskin. He had no feeling, and no volitional motor function from the waist down. He was fed intravenously and he was catheterized every three hours to carry the waste from his body.

And then, the day before surgery, there was slight movement in his legs, and he could discern slight feeling in the soles of his feet when the "pizza cutter" was run across them. Chris was heartened and encouraged.

A steady stream of visitors occupied his time during the long wait. He recalls that most of his waking hours were spent with friends and colleagues. Judge Choy, for whom Chris clerked, was a member of the Christian Businessmen's Association, and he and his group often came to the hospital to pray at Chris' bedside.

Friends with whom Chris played poker continued their ritual of cards. "They would pull up a table to the bed, and we'd play just like we normally do.

Of course, I was totally drugged at the time, so I have no idea how much money I lost to them," he laughed.

Chris also continued to work. His job was to write legal opinions for the judge, and briefs were brought in for him to read. He read while on his back, and during the period of time when he was relegated to his left side, he wrote.

Doctors labored to repair the splintered back and reconnect severed nerves and muscles. A graft was taken from his hip to form a living mortar with which to fuse the vertebrae. The quadricep muscle in his right leg was beyond repair, and had to be removed. Chris lay in his hospital bed after surgery awaiting the prognosis.

The success of the surgery could not be gauged for several days. Finally, the doctors began to assess their work. The slight sensations he had felt in his legs just prior to the surgery had disappeared. "I was fairly equanimous about being paralyzed before I felt movement. But then after having had some sort of hope, and then having it taken from me, I was not pleased."

The paralysis, however, was short-lived. In a matter of days Chris began feeling sensations . . . hot, cold, pain. The jagged pizza cutter finally elicited a scream. The surgeons had successfully reconstructed and rewired the tangled mess that was Chris' back. The skilled hands of the surgeons had done their work. Now it was up to Chris and to the healing powers of his own body to recover.

His first steps were those of a baby. His control over the nerves in his muscles was rudimentary, and the world as he knew it before the accident now existed only as far as his hands hung to his sides. He was given a grasping tool to help him with such simple tasks as reaching for a book or pulling on socks, tasks which took him weeks to master. And yet he wanted desperately to do things as normally as possible.

The first day home, in the company of his father and Mike Cook, he fell over when merely reaching for a book lying on the coffee table. "I remember having an argument with him about that," said his father, Charles Cox. "Not that he was trying to do something normally, but that he was trying to do it without some sort of support, such as leaning against a wall."

Chris responds matter-of-factly. "The coffee table wasn't near a wall."

The brace of steel bars and leather straps which encased Chris' body made normal mobility impossible. He was obliged to purchase a new wardrobe of clothes several sizes larger to accommodate the bulk, in a stretch fabric he had sworn he "would never wear." After a short recovery period at home, Chris was anxious to return to work. But sitting at his desk would be an impossibility with the cumbersome brace and the immobility it provided. The General Services Administration built for Chris a stand-up desk where he could work in the only position available to him other than lying down.

His recovery was startlingly rapid. Six months later, he decided he didn't need the brace any more, and he "just got rid of it." Just twenty-six weeks earlier he was fighting for his life and facing the prospect of living his life paralyzed from the waist down.

After finishing his term with Judge Choy, Chris went to the law firm of Latham and Watkins in Newport Beach, California, where he was soon to become the youngest partner in the firm's history. In 1982 he took a leave of absence for a guest professorship in tax law at the Harvard School of Business.

In 1986, he took another leave of absence to become Senior Associate Counsel to President Ronald Reagan in the White House. His stand-up desk went with him. On February 1, 1988, he resigned his position to run for Congress, and in June of that year won a hotly contested primary for what is considered by many conservatives to be the United States' plum district.

What was it inside Christopher Cox that made him a survivor? From what hidden wells was he able to draw the strength to pull himself, paralyzed, blinded, and in agonizing pain, from underneath that jeep? Why did he not succumb to the blessed relief of unconsciousness? And once freed, what gave him the will to live, and to recover so remarkably from his devastating injuries? What qualities does Chris possess that allowed him to swim with such strength against the current that would have swept under so many?

Exercises for Confidence

1) Relax your muscles. When you are upset your muscles automatically tense up.

2) Deliberately *place* thoughts of calmness in your mind. A tranquil beach. A secluded forest. A misty dawn.

3) Ask yourself specific questions. "What, exactly, do I feel unsure of about myself?" _____

   _____

   _____

   Do not settle for vague answers. Saying "I can't cope" is not sufficient. Pinpoint your uncertainty. "I am afraid that I will lose my composure in front of everyone and I will be embarrassed" is a much more proper assessment. By identifying the specific problem, you can work on specific solutions.

4) Ask yourself how important is the immediate fear that you described in #3?

   _____

   _____

   What is the worst that could happen?_____

   _____

   _____

   _____

5) Determine if the problem is a permanent one or temporary one. ("I lost my house in a fire" is really temporary. Being without a home is changeable.)

6) What can you do about the problem/fear?*Be specific!* ("I can move in with friends until the insurance settlement. Then, I can rebuild the house.")

   _____

   _____

7) Practice confident self-image visualization techniques. *See* yourself as a well person. *See* yourself as independent, going out to the store, returning to work. Watch yourself in your mind's eye telling the victimizer—"No more." Hear the words.

8) Physically act the part of the image you want. To portray confidence, keep your chin level with the ground or slightly upturned. Look people straight in the eye. Do not peer upwards from under your eyebrows with a downturned head. Unclench your hands and your jaw muscles. Confident people have a relaxed, unhurried demeanor. Slow down your words; enunciate clearly. Consciously lower the pitch of your voice. Smile if appropriate. (Practice these techniques when you are not under stress, so they will be more easily called upon later.)

9) Surround yourself with the people and things that reinforce your desired self-image. If your desired self-image is one of health and strength, seek out healthy people and healthy settings. Get out of bed and outside. If your desired self-image is one of peace and serenity, your living arrangements should reflect that — cool colors, plants, no clutter, etc., spend time with serene people.

10) Dress the part. If your desired self-image is of financial success, dress successfully. For health, get out of the hospital gown or the terry cloth robe. Shower, shave, do your hair. Do your makeup. To see the influence our mode of dress exerts, go through the following list and ascribe a label (image) to the person who is wearing the following:
   - A torn t-shirt with an obscene slogan;
   - A three-piece pinstrip suit;
   - A silk blouse with pearls;
   - A long denim skirt and cotton blouse;
   - A polyester leisure suit;
   - A leather miniskirt, tanktop, spike heels;
   - A flannel shirt, jeans, and work boots;
   - A polo shirt, tennis shorts, and tennis shoes; Hawaiian-print shirt, cutoff jeans, and sandals.

Like it or not, clothes are symbols in our society. In effect, the medium is the message.

Chapter Five

HEART

Don't wait for heroes. Believe in yourself, you've got the power. Winners are losers who gave it just one more try.
Dennis DeYoung

I like the term "Heart." It reaches into the soul of a Champion and captures the spirit, the flame that burns within. It is in the heart of a Champion where we find courage, endurance, spirit, and determination.

Without the heart, where is the life? The heart is what keeps us going. The ancient Greeks and Romans believed that the heart was the organ of our emotions. All love, feeling, and passion emitted from the heart. Even today, we describe people as having a "heart of gold," or a "heart of stone." We use such terms as "heartsick," "broken heart," "heart to heart talks," and a "heavy heart."

There is more intuitive understanding about "heart" than scientific fact. And yet, heart — courage, endurance, spirit, and determination — emerges again and again as a common quality of Champions. As Dennis DeYoung says above, it is the courage and determination to fight to stay afloat in the face of adversity, no matter how hard it tries to knock you down.

Who can say just what courage is, and who can determine who is courageous? Is the much-decorated war hero more courageous than the widow of the man he killed? We can only see what courage does. In the Champion, courage is that strength of heart which propels a person to endure that which seems unendurable, or to do that which seems impossible. It is the glue which holds our minds and bodies together when the forces of adversity would break them apart.

In looking at Champions in whom courage is evident, we see its power, but we cannot extract its essence for our use. As John F. Kennedy said in *Profiles in Courage,* "The stories of past courage can define that ingredient — they can teach, they can offer hope, they can provide inspiration. But they cannot supply courage itself. For this each man must look into his own soul."

A Champion's heart is forged of courage under the heat of fear.

My own feelings when I battled with cancer were mirrored by Dr. John A. MacDonald. A general surgeon who had often had to tell patients of a malignancy, MacDonald found himself facing the dreaded pronouncement of cancer. In his book *When Cancer Strikes* (1979), MacDonald describes the self-pity that washed over him at first, and then the awakening of determination to win.

"When you begin to rally, to stop feeling sorry for yourself, you are really beginning to battle your cancer. This is when we as psychologists hear patients say, 'I won't give up.'"

Having lost his first wife to leukemia and facing his own mortality, MacDonald nevertheless fought with courage. In his book, he cites 18th century dramatist Vittorio Alfieri, who said, "Often the test of courage is not to die, but to live." MacDonald explains that "living with cancer engenders more than pressure; it begets terror. To live with it, to face up to it — *that's* courage."

When he realized the imminence of his mortality, MacDonald grew to cherish each precious moment of his remaining days with a heightened awareness and appreciation.

It takes tremendous courage to battle dragons. In MacDonald's case, the dragon was cancer. And this time, the dragon won. Shortly after writing his book, MacDonald died. But John MacDonald was a Champion, for though he lost his battle with cancer, he slew his dragon of fear.

Sometimes the courage we've built up slowly and painfully to survive a tragedy provides us the very resources we need to deal with a subsequent, unrelated crisis.

Such is the case of Sergeant Kenneth Pollock, a Maryland State Police officer, whose sixteen-year-old son, Jeffrey, had died in Pollock's arms, the victim of a motorcycle accident. The courage Pollock had developed in dealing with his own son's death enabled him to place himself between a speeding car and a van carrying David and Laura Cannon and their infant daughter. Three cars were demolished, and there were injuries, but thanks to Pollock there were no fatalities. "I'm so pleased that the Cannons didn't have to suffer the horror that I went through losing a child," Pollock said in explaining his deliberate decision to spare others the personal tragedy he had endured.

Adversity prepared me for more than one upstream journey. My refusal to be defeated by the cancer strengthened my determination to withstand any adversity. Losing a part of myself to cancer and the surgeon's knife also oddly prepared me for a more deeper personal loss, my divorce. Much like my cancer, I felt that this could not be happening to me, because of the love I so deeply felt for my wife and children. I felt myself losing control over the situation. After all, I had my life plan all figured out. I was working very hard, six to seven days a week, because that is what my greatest role model, my father, did and I thought that was what a husband, and a father, was supposed to do. I thought that working harder would enable me to buy my wife some nicer clothes, live in a nicer house, and send my children to a nicer school. However, by spending so much time being a good provider, I failed to work at my relationships with my wife and two children.

The death of a marriage is just like the death of a loved one, we seem to go through the same type of grief responses; shock, guilt, depression, and anger. I knew I had within me the courage to go on, and the burning desire to learn to adapt, within my limits and to the best of my ability, from the deepest loss I think that I will have ever endured. I knew that I had the heart to go on and create a new life of love and joy. By realizing that I was unable to salvage the romantic relationship with my wife, I focused my attention and energy on becoming the best possible "daddy" to my children. Before the divorce I was their "father," but now I have learned and I have become their "daddy."

I feel that I had a second chance at life in surviving cancer, and whatever courage I had during my ordeal made me stronger and more determined to truly savor my second life. The divorce does not change that.

I was touched by the story of Uli Derickson, the courageous woman aboard the hijacked TWA flight 847 in 1985. In the face of death, she bravely, and with dignity, endured the terrifying ordeal, putting her fear aside to help the frightened and the wounded. She, too, felt that she was given a second life by surviving. Israeli friends told her that after going through such an ordeal, you get to add an extra word to your name — *haya* — which means life.

In every Champion there is a sense of life. As Martin Luther King, Jr. said, "Courageous men never lose their zest for living even though their life situation is zestless; cowardly men, overwhelmed by the uncertainties of life, lose the will to live."

Alexis Carrel also sees the quality of heart as evidence of a passion for life.

"The sacrifice of one's self is not very difficult for one burning with passion for a great adventure." Such is the stuff of courage which enables people to overcome their fears in order that they may live more fully.

Actor Jerry Lewis talks about "his kids," the victims of muscular dystrophy, with a sense of wonder for their sense of life. "You see courage in its most beautiful sense and they have such a passion for life — a passion that they know will be taken from them. Yet that passion grows and each day of their lives they think positive and uplifting thoughts."

Of the quality of courage Jerry sees in "his kids," he says, "I truly believe it's God's compensation. I think when the good Lord looks down on these stricken human beings, he has to say to himself: 'Let me give them something good to make up for the bad' . . . and much of that good that He gives them is courage, fight, energy, enthusiasm, dreams, and hope."

The literature of American sport is rich with the stories of athletes who began with physical resources flimsier than the average person who deems it an effort to climb a flight of stairs. Armed with more heart than sinew, these athletes illustrate the magic powers that desire and determination can have on the most paltry raw material.

Take a skinny little kid with rickets, add heart, and you have an O.J. Simpson. Take a desperately poor black child from Alabama, unable to even walk because of a huge growth on his leg, add heart, and you have a Jesse Owens. Take a young child paralyzed by polio, add heart, and you have a Ray Ewry, winner of ten gold medals spanning four Olympiads. Take a child born with only half a right foot, add heart, and you have a Tom Dempsey who holds the NFL record for the longest field goal kicked (sixty-three yards). Take a crippled little girl from Tennessee in metal leg braces, add heart, and you have a Wilma Rudolph. "The difference between the impossible and the possible lies in a man's determination," observes Dodger's manager Tommy Lasorda.

Kitty O'Neil was born deaf. If that were not enough adversity to cope with in a world designed for the hearing, Kitty was crippled with spinal meningitis. As an adult, she is a cancer survivor, thanks to two operations.

Simply living independently and productively is an upstream journey for many, but that was not enough for Kitty.

Taught by her adversities how to endure and persevere, Kitty chose the remarkable life of risk and adventure as a Hollywood stuntwoman. She performed the action scenes for the stars; being drowned, set afire, dangled from windows, shoved off cliffs and generally abused on a daily basis. She later went on to set the women's land speed record in a characteristic venture into the unknown, always testing the limits and living her life with Heart.

Determination is a powerful component of Heart. The desire to overcome distinguishes the Champion.

My daughter Sarah, age eight, has taught me a lot about courage and determination. At the age of four she had difficulty walking and my wife and I took her to the doctor. He told us that she had perioneal muscles missing in her right foot. These missing muscles have the responsibility of holding her right foot up. Without these muscles she often walks with a slight limp, and must wear a brace. Amid the ridicule she endured from her classmates, Sarah was determined to be just like all of the other children her age. I can remember seeing her climb up the pine tree in our back yard when none of her other friends would. I must admit, though, that watching her proudly climb the tree and sway in the breeze was not good on my heart. Sarah let me in on her secret one evening about a year ago when I came home from work and asked her how her day was. She told me that she had run in several races that day. I quickly developed a lump in my throat in anticipation of what to say to my daughter to help her through what I believed was another heartbreaking experience for her. She realized quickly that I was trying to hold back my tears to help and support her through what I believed was a trying time for her. With her pretty brown eyes she smiled at me and said, "Daddy, you know I won a few of those races today!" As I sat there with my eyes moistened she continued, "Daddy, I just had to try harder than the other kids." Indeed, my Sarah has taught me a lot about heart.

For a Republican trying to win a Senate seat in an historically Democratic district, political affiliation can be adversity enough. But Bob Ryan became just the third Republican to do so in over fifty years when he won the Las Vegas area Senate in 1983. Bob Ryan is blind.

"We all have personal difficulties of some kind," he says "I wanted a job that would say to people, 'Hey, look what a totally sightless person can do.'"

In *Tough Times Never Last But Tough People Do!* (1983), Robert Schuller describes his boyhood on a midwestern farm during the Great Depression. The family farm was on the brink of foreclosure because of the drought, when a tornado sucked away any remaining hope. He saw twenty-six years of his parents' labor destroyed in minutes. But what he saw later would stay in his mind more vividly than the destruction: the faithful determination of his father to rebuild; from a $50 section of home scheduled for demolition came a new family homestead. Schuller remembers the slogan on a calendar from the town bank in Iowa: "Great people are ordinary people with extraordinary amounts of determination."

Jeff Blatnick's refusal to give up and accept his cancer was the fighting spirit and determination that won him both his life and the gold medal in Greco-Roman wrestling in the 1984 Olympics.

Joseph Blank tells the story of Mary Groda-Lewis in the July 1986 issue of *Reader's Digest*. She was an elementary school drop-out, street fighter and juvenile offender whose formative years were plagued by dyslexia, poverty, and the loss of the family home. Mary Groda-Lewis nevertheless was a Champion. The young single parent of two children fought back after five cardiac arrests and a stroke which required her to learn to read, write and talk all over again. She attended school in the afternoon and worked 4:00 A.M. til noon to support her children. Today, she is a medical doctor.

This grueling upstream journey graphically illustrates the quality of heart so apparent in Champions. With every societal excuse in the book, Mary could have easily decided to take the easier, downstream route. But she didn't. She was determined and persistent. Her fighting spirit which had gotten her into trouble as an adolescent was now her ally, and she used it to her advantage. She refused to be defeated by either circumstance or her own shortcomings.

Often, the courage that a Champion is able to muster comes as a surprise. Most of the time, the situation which demands the most heart is not planned for, and the Champion finds himself having to call upon part of himself he never knew existed.

Monica Dickens, in her book *Miracles of Courage* (1985), talks about the mothers of gravely ill children and the pain they must bear. She shares their thoughts on how they summon the strength and courage to maintain their bedside vigils with their children. "People tell me that I'm strong. I'm not, you just do as much as you can. What else is there to do? Sometimes you're exhausted and you say 'I don't want to do this anymore.' So you look around to see who else is going to do it and there's no one but you," said Dickens.

"People say it only happens to those who are strong enough to bear it. That's not true. You get strong because it has happened!"

As President John F. Kennedy wrote, "To be courageous requires no exceptional qualifications, no magic formula, no special combination of time, place, and circumstance. It is an opportunity that sooner or later is presented to us all."

Actress Theresa Saldana's life was thrust into a test of courage and determination on a May afternoon in 1982, when she survived a vicious knife attack by a maniacal fan. She echoes the feeling of a renewed sense of life that she gained from the chilling ordeal. "When you come out of the other side of tragedy, there's a real ecstasy that you get into," she told journalist Michael Ryan. "When something happens that knocks you that far down, the natural momentum — if you allow it to happen and don't let yourself get stuck down there — that pendulum swing is pretty high."

Her courage and determination to savor her second life is evidenced by what she has been doing since the attack. A book, three movies, victims' rights groups, political activism and plenty of time to smell the roses. "The fact that I have been in such a perilous position—the attack, the recovery, being an invalid for a long period of time — makes me really relish the good things in my life," she says. "Today, just being able to go to dance class, and go to aerobics and have freedom and movie jobs. . . . I appreciate them on a different level than before."

Such a zeal for life is the product of the heart that endured, and perhaps the prize for having endured.

Champions such as Derikson, McDonald, and Saldana saw something upstream worth fighting for. Through the wearying battle against the current, they persevered. And once they arrived they were not disappointed. The journey itself made the destination sweeter.

You've been reading about Champions who had Heart. In the following pages, you'll meet Frank Epperson, a Champion who didn't let a wheelchair get in the way of his dreams. Then go back to your quiet place and discover the Heart of the Champion within you.

HEART

Something to Think About and Do

At twenty-two years of age, Frank Epperson had reached a plateau many do not even dare to dream. He went to Seoul, Korea, to compete in the 1988 Summer Olympic Games in five different events. Frank is a sprinter, and competed in the 100, 200, and 400K sprints, as well as the 4-by-100 relay and slalom obstacle events. He won a medal in each event; two silver and two bronze.

The dark haired young man with the intense eyes looks more like a body-builder than a sprinter. In fact, he bench presses 230 pounds, exactly twice his weight. You see, most of his body weight is above his waist. If his legs were proportionate to his body, Frank would be well over six feet tall. But he is just 5' 6".

Frank Epperson was born with spina bifida, a congenital cleft of the spine caused by the failure of the two parts of the spine to fuse during the course of his development. Consequently, he is paralyzed from the waist down.

Frank competes in running events in his wheelchair. A familiar face on the Midwestern circuit, he excels in both sprints and marathon length events. From the time he was thirteen, Frank raced. Unable to compete on foot, he straps himself into his wheelchair and pushes, both mentally and physically.

He won three bronze medals in his first international competition in 1987 at the Stoke-Mandevil World Games in Britain and he said they "just made me hungry." So he headed off to the Windsor Classic Indoor Games for the Physically Disabled in Ontario just months later, adding more medals to the already burgeoning collection.

In his mere twenty-two years, Frank has faced ten surgeries, many of which took place when he was seven and eight years old. When the other children his age were nursing scraped knees and bruised shins from climbing trees and playing Little League ball, Frank was enduring excruciating procedures his young mind could not comprehend. Summer vacation for some meant fishing and camp. For Frank, it meant Riley Children's Hospital in Indianapolis.

As a teenager, Frank watched as the other kids paired off, waiting and wondering when he would find that special girl. He resented the presumption that only a girl somehow "flawed" would be interested in him — someone less pretty, less smart, or less fun to be with.

Being confined to a wheelchair is not his only challenge. "Attitudes are the biggest barrier," he said. "If it's a physical barrier, I can just hammer away at it until I break it down. But you can't just dynamite an attitude."

From his infancy Frank experienced life very differently than other children. While the children cruised the cul-de-sac in Big Wheels and tricycles, Frank sat in a wheelchair.

One of the basic needs of a child is a sense of belonging. It is painful enough for a child growing up, as he seeks his place among his peers, dreading the stigma of being different. For a boy in a wheelchair, it is devastating.

But Frank has survived the cruelty of childhood and adolescence. He has survived better than many of us, for whom the taunts and the jeers were aimed at our clothes or our lunch boxes, and not at our very selves. Not only has he survived, he has conquered. Still for Frank, each day must be conquered anew, with ever increasing foes and new battlefields.

It is not enough that the physical education major has a lifetime of uphill challenges. Frank Epperson chooses a literal uphill course on the cross country terrains he tackles in sanctioned competition.

What is it within Frank that gives him the capacity for such achievement? Why is he not content to be a spectator of life like so many others, many of whom are able-bodied? What was he able to reach for deep inside of himself and pull out when it would have been so much easier not to? He has heart!

Exercises on Heart

1) Think back to an incident or setback that was something you really wanted, or something that you gave up on. What was the incident? _____

   _____

   _____

   _____

   _____

   _____

2) As you look back on the incident now, what additional things might you have tried to make the situation turn out more favorably? _____

   _____

   _____

   _____

   _____

3) If the same incident were to happen today, what might you do the same or differently in order to increase your self-esteem? _____

   _____

   _____

   _____

   _____

4) Write a letter to yourself then, telling yourself what you would have liked to hear that would have given you the Heart to persevere. _____

   _____

   _____

   _____

   _____

Chapter Six

ADAPTABILITY

We can't direct the wind, but we can adjust the sails.

Unknown

Adaptability — the ability to switch gears and roll with the punches, the ability to "adjust the sails," is a basic component of a Champion.

"Rolling with the punches" is such an oft used cliché, we may overlook how very valuable this advice is. Skilled stuntmen routinely replace the star in a Hollywood fight scene. Why? Because they know how to fall without hurting themselves. They roll with it, and in the rolling diffuse the shock. They let the motion of their entire body absorb and then dissipate the impact. Unskilled in rolling with the punches, the star would fall, stiff and rigid, extending an arm to brace himself. The full force of the impact would be concentrated in his arm. Unable to absorb the shock by itself, the arm would break.

Inflexibility can break you. The old adage about the willow tree bending in a storm and being able to survive intact applies to people as well. When the storm of adversity hits, the Champion bends.

The same adaptability which gets us through a crisis may be the adaptability that can *prevent* a crisis.

"Today, couples whose marriages have lasted fifteen years or more have lived through some of the most rapid social change in history," says Francine Klagsbrun in her book *Married People: Staying Together In The Age Of Divorce*. "New emphasis on a woman's rights outside her home, and on a man's responsibility inside his, have brought tension to many marriages. Other couples, however, have had the flexibility to pick up what was useful to them and incorporate new ideals in their marriage."

Champions apply the principles of physical flexibility to their mental state.

If our minds are locked into one rigid stance, we may not be able to withstand the impact of adversity. Champions provide themselves with mental "Shock Absorbers."

Shock Absorbers

Champions have more than one role. The more roles a person has, the more likely he is to survive a blow. For example, to a woman whose sole role has been wife and mother, losing custody in a divorce case is an attack on her very self. Without other dimensions of self to absorb and dissipate the shock, the entire force of the blow is taken by wife/mother. If she had more roles, say—teacher and artist—she would have other facets of self which could remain intact.

Chris Cox was a victim of a freak jeep accident, who at age twenty-five suddenly became a paraplegic. Chris discussed his paralysis after the jeep accident. "Of course I didn't like it, but it wasn't like I was a runner. I'm a lawyer and you can still be a lawyer from a wheelchair," he says. Chris' multi-faceted experience and talents afforded a multiplicity of roles from which he could draw confidence. He wrote, had business interests, public speaking experience, and a wealth of interest in such diverse topics as politics, travel, sports, and even a pretty fair talent for the piano. Chris had a wide range of roles to support his confidence throughout his ordeal.

The ability and the desire to learn is another of the Champions shock absorbers. To remain flexible and adaptable, the Champion seizes upon every opportunity to learn new skills and new concepts, never knowing when one might come in handy.

The current popular tv network adventure series, "MacGyver," plays upon the improvisational skills of the hero, rather than his brawn. He uses the simplest of resources to serve his purpose. A piece of string, chewing gum, and a light bulb become an ingenious means of escape. While occasionally farfetched, the series illustrates the value of being able to improvise, to see the resources at hand in a new light.

The animal and plant kingdom is a perfect example of adaptability in action. Take lichen, a mosslike plant which can survive for thousands of years. It owes its survival to its adaptability — doing things other plants cannot. Some plants in nitrogen-poor habitats adapt by changing their diet. No nitrogen? Well, they just become carnivorous. Pitcher plants, Butterworts, and the Venus flytrap flourish in near sterile conditions because they weren't too set in their ways.

Champions do the same thing. They are not locked into one way of looking at or of doing something. Louis Braille rethought the concept of reading and adapted the printed word to a code of raised dots which could be "seen" by touch.

Surgeon Francisco Bucio was buried under the rubble of the Mexico City earthquake in 1985. He was trapped for four days without food and water, and yet he survived. But surviving with his life was not to be the only miracle. What happened next was even more incredible. Bucio's fingers had to be amputated in the rescue procedure; the price exacted for his life would be his career. But Dr. Harry Buncke at the Davies Medical Center in San Francisco had other ideas, ideas he had gotten from watching paralyzed artists who adapt by using their toes to grip the paint brush. Buncke grafted Bucios toes to his hands. After learning the dexterity in a miraculous adaptive process, Bucio is now a plastic surgeon bringing new life and hope, just as it had been brought to him.

The deaf learn new languages — sign language and lip reading. Diabetics adapt to new diets and daily insulin injections. People in chronic pain learn how to "shut off" the sensors, and to block out pain.

These are all learned skills, not innate. The more flexible and open to learning that we are before a crisis hits, the more prepared we are to meet adversity.

In Hyatt and Gottlieb's book *When Smart People Fail*, the distinction is made between learners and nonlearners. Learners, the authors maintain, are able to pull themselves out of their setbacks because of the knowledge gained from the experience.

I like that. Each setback provides its own set of data that the learners can store away for future reference.

As discussed earlier, I made several mistakes with my wife and children. I thought I was doing right by working long, hard hours to earn extra money to have a little nicer house for them, to send my children to a little nicer school, and to treat my wife to some of the extravagances of life. However, in looking back, I now see how I did not pay the proper attention to my wife and children, thus leading to the death of my marriage. I, like Hyatt and Gottlieb's "learners," gained widsom and knowledge from the setback of my divorce. I realized that it was too late to save my marriage, but it was not too late to be a good, loving "daddy" to my children. I also realized that the mistake of trying so hard to make sure that my wife and children would have many of the nicer things in life had led me to forget the one thing they wanted most to have, "me." But I have learned, I know now that my children have a loving "daddy" who is there for them more emotionally than financially. Additionally, I hope someday to remarry and be a much better and loving husband. All this means that from adversity we learn from our mistakes. We learn that we can't undo that which is done, but we learn that we can be the best person that we can be by trying not to make the same mistake again.

Learning from our mistakes is not just a coping technique or an optimistic viewpoint of failure. Learning from our mistakes is a far more efficient way of learning.

Problem-Solving—Creativity

A key component in a Champion's adaptability is effective problem-solving. Problem-solving is no more than coming up with a new way of looking at something. This is the essence of creativity.

When we think of the creative person we usually think of sculptors, painters, or writers. Our perception is that they "create" a work, and we marvel at their genius, knowing that this is an inherent ability, a gift from God that we simply do not have. This is only partially correct.

True, some people do seem to have an inborn "gift" for music, art, or writing. But we limit ourselves when we dismiss the possibility that we, too, have the ability to be creative.

The writer does not create words. He rearranges words. The sculptor does not create a statue. He removes pieces of stone from a large rock. The painter does not create a landscape. She applies areas of color to a canvas, rearranging existing oil and pigment to her own purposes.

Kahlil Gibran described the creative nature of man as being a gift from God. He "left electricity in the clouds" for us to discover so that we may share in the divine joy of creation. Seeing the possibilities. Moving the pieces around to come up with a new masterpiece. This is problem-solving, and we cannot do this if we see only what we have always seen.

Creativity then is simply looking at something with a different eye, rearranging existing things or circumstances for our own purposes. This is the essence of problem-solving and it is the heart of adaptability.

Adversity has a peculiar way of confronting us so that we see only the blocked path. We don't see the options, the alternate routes. Champions, however, have the ability to see those alternate routes because of their creative, problem-solving qualities.

"My disability is one of the greatest advantages I have," contends dyslexic Kathy Kolbe. "It helped me become a student of the thinking process before I was even in kindergarten."

Kolbe is today CEO of the firm Resources for the Gifted, a company she launched on $500 and now grosses $3.5 million annually. As a student and master of the "thinking process," Kolbe survived the first years of setbacks — fires, embezzling employees, and divorce — with the same resources she was peddling to gifted students. "I never, never feel overwhelmed," she says. "I enjoy a challenge." The adaptable Champion finds ways to use the special insight of adversity.

Blinded in a playground accident at age ten, Peter Duran went on to public high school, Trinity College, and the University of Illinois. A post graduate student in psycholinguistics, Peter's abilities and energies were turned toward developing the first talking computer, a boon to other nonsighted people who wanted to use computers. Later, he went on to develop a computer that reads Braille aloud.

A very dear friend of mine, Joe Elliot, unlike Peter, was blinded from birth. But like Peter and other Champions, Joe did not let his blindness obstruct his childhood dream of becoming a disc jockey and radio talk show host. When asked how he overcame the numerous obstacles and learned how to operate all of the complicated electronic gadgetry of a radio station Joe said, "You do what you want to do if it is important to you." He said that he believes that anyone can do whatever he or she wants to do within the realm of possibilities. Joe says that his perspective on life can be summed up best by his favorite quote by Woody Allen. Woody says, "Ninety percent of life is just showing up."

Dr. Vaillant, in his book about the study, *Adaption to Life,* found several common denominators among the successful. But in an interview in *People* magazine (December 5, 1977), Vaillant credits the crucial role of defense mechanisms as the sine qua non of success. "When confronted by conflict," he says, "they engaged in unconscious but often creative behavior. Various styles of adapting allowed them to carry on life's business without anxiety or depression."

Of the coping mechanisms, Vaillant was most intrigued with what he calls "sublimation," a redirecting of energies into another pursuit or challenge, usually combining the adversity with a previous passion.

Roger Withrow was an expert rifle marksman. In 1976 he won the title of National High Power Champion-Marksman Class. In 1978 he led his team from Murray State University in Kentucky to the National Collegiate Small Bore Team Championship, and led the 2nd Region ROTC team to the National Championship in the Infantry Trophy match. The Pan American Games and the 1980 Olympics were well within his range. But, in the fall of 1978 Roger developed a herniated disc, and dropped out of school.

This was only a minor setback for the intense young man with his goals set to be the best marksman in the world. But on May 7, 1979, Roger felt his dreams crash down on him when he was injured on a coal mining site while working for his father's construction company. After almost thirty-five surgeries Roger was paralyzed from the waist down, confined to a wheelchair. After many weeks of recuperation, including six weeks on an open psychiatric unit, Roger came to realize that he would never walk again, but he swore that that would be his only limitation. He began his shooting career again, and won the gold medal in the VII Pan American Wheelchair Games.

Roger is a perfect example of Vaillant's sublimation theory. Roger's passion was shooting, and then the accident left him out of contention. But Roger adapted by combining his adversity with his passion to spearhead the wheelchair athlete movement in shooting, quickly regaining world-class status.

One of the most destructive forces in our lives is anger. It is also one of the most common. Anger frequently appears as an initial response to adversity and tragedy. Often it is unfocused and lashes out randomly in a knee-jerk reaction to the inexplicable unfairness of life.

What distinguishes the Champion, however, is the ability to harness that power and energy and adapt it toward good. Mary Lenaghan turned her blind rage at the senseless death of her son in a fraternity hazing into a sharply focused action plan. She channeled her anger into a successful effort to push for an anti-hazing law in the Massachusetts State Legislature.

Similarly, Candy Lightner's frustration with a system that did not punish drunk drivers who kill, led her to mix anger and grief into an explosive and effective reaction. Candy's anger after the death of her daughter Cari at the hands of a drunk driver was the moving force behind the formation of the hugely successful group called Mothers Against Drunk Driving (MADD).

I remember sitting in my hospital bed after my cancer surgery feeling sorry for myself and hoping that my University of Louisville teaching colleagues and students were doing the same. I was throwing a "Let's Feel Sorry for Stan" party and I was hoping that everybody else was going to join in. I was very angry for being diagnosed with a possibly fatal disease at such a young age, and for having to live the rest of my life with a constant reminder of that awful day. It seemed like all my energy was turned inward, feeding my self-pity and anger. Five days after the surgery I began concentrating my focus on getting better and overcoming this possibly fatal setback in my life. I quickly realized that the first thing to do was redirect my energy. I had to channel my inward energy outward to place my focus in the healthier direction, recovery. I began writing journal articles about my recent experiences. On the seventh day after surgery I returned to the University to teach, and I actually hit fielding practice to the university baseball team. I know what you are saying . . . "Not a very intelligent move on my part," but at least my pity party was over and I was focusing my energy externally on the path to a quick and successful recovery.

The Champion does not get bogged down with minor irritations. The little annoyances of life do not get to him because he is flexible enough to deal with them, or to ignore them completely.

If we cannot be flexible enough to deal with minor things, what will the major things do to us?

In fact, learning to roll with the daily hassles may be the best preparation we can have for the major adversities. In fact it is our peevish qualities that cause us so much stress.

Minor hassles are better predictors of illness rates than are major events. Everyday paperwork caused more health problems for police officers than the comparatively major stresses of apprehending criminals.

One of the reasons we as a society experience so much stress is our inability to adapt. We let the minor aggravations of life get to us as much as we do the major challenges. In fact, we could be better major league players than we are minor league players.

A mother of three teenagers confessed to me that she flew off the handle on a daily basis over her sons' bickering, sloppiness, and sassiness. It was causing her a great deal of stress, and certainly wasn't helping out the family situation. To her surprise, she handled a serious situation in a calm, reassured manner. When one of her boys was suspended for cheating, she took control and rationally discussed the situation with the boy and the school principal. While this situation was far more serious, she experienced less stress handling this incident than she did with the everyday aggravations.

We do this every day. We let complete strangers, people whom we neither know nor care about, cause us to be uptight, anxious, surly, or annoyed. The fellow in the supermarket express checkout line with sixteen items and a third-party check gets more of our energy than our spouse who needs to talk after a bad day. The pushy telephone solicitor, instead of stealing just thirty seconds from our day commands minutes, even hours, of our energy as we fret and fume and recount our aggravation to whomever will listen. This is nonsense.

Adapt! If you can't adapt enough to hang up the phone with a cheery, "No, thank you," or learn to expect an occasional delay at the supermarket or bank, then adapting to a crisis may be a severe tax on your limits. But as the mother of the teenagers illustrated, we probably do have these coping skills, but we usually don't call on them for everyday situations. We keep them in reserve for the "important" things.

All of us have had the experience of having to deal with a crisis and surprising ourselves with our cool. Then, when the immediate danger is over, we "go to pieces." We do this precisely because we know when we must cope and when we don't have to. As one woman put it, "When my husband's home, I scream for him to come and kill the creepy, crawly thing in the bathroom. When he's out of town I just squash it with my shoe."

You do what you have to do. Our inability to adapt to change is a major factor in stress. Change is represented by everything from a divorce, to death, to the seemingly inconsequential. A change of office furniture has been known to throw employees into a tizzy. A detour on your normal route to work, a plane flight delay, or a rainstorm on your golf day can be as stressful as waiting to hear the results of your CPA exams. Why?

Mostly because of our inability to distinguish between a real threat and an imagined one. Our ancestral "fight or flight" instinct goes into operational mode automatically. Our rapidly changing society has out-paced our evolutionary changes. We experience the physiological changes that characterize this instinct and call it "stress." We can learn to override this instinct, however. A conscious effort must be made to do this.

As I pointed out earlier, all the qualities of a Champion inter-relate. We talked about Confidence being evidenced by the absence of stress. Well, stress is basically the inability to adapt, so if our Adaptability Quotient is deficient, our

Confidence suffers as well.

What can we do to insulate ourselves from the pesky slings and arrows of everyday life? What kinds of things can we do to "hassle proof" our lives?

Developing skills of adaptability is a matter of un-learning all the structured mental processes we learned in school. While we learned to read, write, and do mathematical problems, we also lost our ability to see things in creative ways. We were taught that there is a "right way" to do everything, and consequently we became conditioned to see only one way. We grow up learning that there is one answer to every problem. Many important issues are not so cut and dry. By looking for a second or third answer we can provide alternatives to a dilemma.

Remember as a child how you used to be obsessed with what-if's? "What if there was a snowstorm and I couldn't get to school? What if the snow went past the windows and covered up the door? Would the lights still work? We could melt snow for the dog's water dish." You saw not problems, but possibilities. An adult, faced with the barrage of what-if's, usually admonishes the child to stop the nonsense — it will never happen anyway — and to get busy on something "useful," like picking up his room.

The adult's creative atrophy is never so evident as when he presents a toddler with a new toy. Fascinated with the myriad of possibilities, the child gleefully embarks on a creative expedition, unhampered by someone else's edict on what this toy is supposed to do. The adult, programmed to the one-way school of thought, officiously takes over, and shows the toddler the "right way" to play with the toy. After repeatedly having her creativity thwarted, the child eventually learns to suppress her natural tendencies. They are further sublimated by teachers who insist she use her right hand, and parents who point out that carrots and peanut butter don't go together, no matter how much the child may like it.

Psychologist and philosopher William Stern noticed this trend during his work in the first quarter of this century. He observed the loss of creativity in adults by saying, "The play of adults . . . is well-nigh devoid of imagination; forms of solitary amusement like collecting have their course laid out for them . . . Social games (cards, tables games, sporting games) are hedged by such a mass of fixed rules that very limited freedom of action remains to creative imagination." How sad that we should no longer even know how to play!

The winds of change are always blowing. In the following exercises, learn how your Adaptability Quotient will allow you to change the rigging on your sails to harness the power of change.

ADAPTABILITY

Something to Think About and Do

The first time I saw my colostomy I felt that, unlike the mythical Phoenix, I would never rise again. That was during my post-operative confinement, while I was still burning in the fires of anguish, pain, fear, and uncertainty. I soon found it ironic to have so many well intentioned people visit me and say, "Well aren't you lucky? You are getting a second chance at life." My response was, "I don't feel lucky. If I were lucky this would not have happened to me. Why me?"

"Why me? Why me?" I repeated over and over. After all, I was at the beginning of my career. I had only recently finished the long, hard, and grinding struggle of earning my doctoral degree in Clinical Psychology from UCLA. Upon receipt of my degree I was offered a teaching job in Louisville, Kentucky and was finally beginning to feel comfortable and settle down. It was during the period of my convalescence that I had time to re-examine my life. I decided that self-pity was useless and unproductive. It was time to check my goals and values and see how I was realizing them. It was a time for restructuring and looking anew at life. I repeatedly asked, "What was I doing?"

With a background in psychology I had worked a lot on who I was. The rethinking of my life and the alteration of my perspective seemed only natural. I was prepared for such adversity by my parents and even by my scoutmaster several years ago. I knew that it was only a matter of time until I would accept that this life threatening disease had invaded my body, and that chances were high that the illness could re-invade my cells at any time.

I began to see other people differently; suddenly the little things they did no longer bothered me. I seemingly had time for everyone — students, secretaries, ballplayers, and coaches. However, what I was not prepared to handle was the daily reminder of my bout with cancer, a colostomy. Before my surgery I was afraid. I did not even know what a colostomy was, but I knew that it was something that I didn't want.

Ten days after surgery I went back to my teaching responsibilities at the University of Louisville and being the assistant coach of the university baseball team. At our own locker room facilities, my self-consciousness was easily handled. Coaches had a private locker room and shower facilities. When we traveled on the road to play other universities things started getting difficult. Typically, visiting team locker rooms are just one large room, with one community shower. I worked overtime at figuring out ways to avoid showering after games until I could get a private bathroom. I did such things as just keeping my trunks on or using gallons of aftershave lotion. After one particularly dusty and musty day, however, there was no way to avoid a good shower at the visiting team locker room. I was certain that seeing my ostomy bag would upset my fellow coaches and the ball players.

My fears were much greater than the realities. To my ball players and coaching colleagues, it couldn't have mattered less. My appliance was seldom noticed or commented upon. My fantasy was that the appliance was twelve inches in circumference, and hanging on a "six foot me." Reality was that my friends on the team respected me, and understood that the colostomy was part of me. It was what I needed to survive.

What a relief to feel like one of the guys again. In fact, the players and coaches became so comfortable with my colostomy that we began occasional good natured kidding. One day during infield practice, while hitting ground balls, the third baseman yelled across to the diamond to me:

"Hey, coach! I hear you also play in the pep band."

Innocently, I responded, "That's right, Keith."

In a flash came back his question: "What do you play, coach . . . bagpipe?"

This kind of freedom to joke and be open with my friends had made coping and adjustment easier.

That was easy, for they were my friends and colleagues. But being a single man was not so easy. Again my imagination worked overtime. Assuredly, I would be sexually repulsive to any young lady who became close to me. Like every man who had just gotten his career on track, there was a readiness on my part to find the right woman. I was ready to start my life as a family man. Because much of my youth was sacrificed to get my doctoral degree, I was ready to start on the next phase of my life. The prevailing thoughts in my mind, however, were, "What woman could possibly love me? Will I be able to make love? Am I still attractive? What will my sexual partner think of my ostomy? Am I dirty?"

Again, my imagination was running wild. I met the woman who would turn out to be my wife and the mother of my two beautiful children. She taught me that a truly sexual relationship is mainly mental and only a small part physical.

What was important was to learn to focus on my communication with her. When I was completely honest and open about my colostomy, I discovered that having a colostomy didn't turn out to be the "big turn off" once thought of. I quickly learned that my wife loved me for what was in my heart, not outwardly for what was on my body. My wife even wrote an article to *The Ostomy Quarterly* stating how close our sexual relationship was and how my appliance was not in any way an interference in our intimate relationship.

Things were great, but then came the divorce that I have spoken of earlier. In my darkest moment, learning to be a good daddy was a powerful lesson to me and others who think nothing good can ever come from something so bad.

EXERCISES TO IMPROVE ADAPTABILITY THROUGH LEARNING

1) Read. Read anything and everything. Each new piece of information you store in your memory bank will add to your savings.

2) Listen. Listen to people around you. Seek out people whom you admire, people whose skills, insight or strengths you wish to emulate. Then listen.

3) Get into the learning habit. Take a class in a foreign language. Brush up on your piano lessons. Subscribe to magazines other than show-biz gossip rags. You see a strange bird on your patio? Find out what it is. There's an earthquake in Paraguay. Find it on the map. Learn something new about Paraguay.

4) De-mystify something that intimidates you. If you feel like a mental midget around cars, get a friend who knows the way around an engine to show you the basics. Intimidated by finance jargon? Insurance matters got you weak-kneed? Sit down with a professional in the field and have him/her walk you through it. Get a glossary of terms which explains the jargon in plain English. No one is born knowing how to fix a leaky toilet or rewire a lamp — plumbers and electricians learned it. So can you.

5) Start building your own home reference library. This need not be expensive. Garage sales, estate auctions, book store clearances, charity book sales, and library sales can all be inexpensive sources — ten cents on the dollar in many cases. Let friends know you want their cast-offs. In clinics you'll still need to use the library, but if you have reference materials at your finger tips, you're more apt to use them immediately. Look for dictionaries, encyclopedias, biographies, atlases, almanacs, travel guides, history, current events, and how-to books. Pick up a book on any subject that interests you. Send for free information from a myriad of government, non-profit, and community service organizations.

6) Use your leisure time to exercise your mind. A pastime need not be a mindless diversion. Do a crossword puzzle. Play word games. See how many words you can make out of the word Champions. Put together a jigsaw puzzle.

7) Ask questions. If you don't understand something, ask to have it explained. The only dumb question is the unasked question. Question your doctor. Ask for an explanation of your bank statement. Ask your mechanic what "adjusting the carburetor" means. Ask your employer why the accounting department follows a particular procedure. Ask your pastor, rabbi, or minister what a particular tenet is based upon.

These exercises will get you into the "learning habit." You will be in the learning mode, which will make you much more receptive to new skills, concepts and ideas, and consequently more adaptable.

We can learn to override instinct to be rigid. You must make a conscious effort to be curious. Using the relaxation exercises discussed in the chapter on confidence, and the exercises in this chapter, will help condition you to a less stressful personality and a broader scope to your life.

EXERCISES ON HOW TO BETTER INSULATE OURSELVES FROM THE EVERYDAY HASSLES OF LIFE

1) Simplify your life. Get rid of the clutter — Throw out the non-essentials. Clean out that closet. Throw away the dust collectors. Get rid of the junk. The Orientals, known for their serenity, create uncluttered surroundings in their homes. Barbara Hemphill, in her book *Taming The Paper Tiger* (1988), believes that "controlling paper will enhance decision-making skills, lessen a sense of guilt, free up your time and energy . . . "

2) Get an answering machine for your phone solicitors so complaining aunts and gossipy neighbors can't steal your precious time.

3) Say "no" to demands on your time unless you really want to commit to something. Do not agree to do something if later you'll resent the time spent.

4) Does traffic get to you? Join a carpool. Leave fifteen minutes earlier. Leave fifteen minutes later. Take a bus.

5) Noise pollution can jangle your nerves. Turn off the TV. Turn down the stereo. Get ear plugs. Send the kids outside. Better yet, you go outside. Turn down the volume on the phone bell. At the office, set aside a quiet-time where typewriters, copy machines, adding machines and chatter are shut off. Call it a mental-health break.

6) Anticipate a hassle, and diffuse it before it can happen. Keep up on routine car and appliance maintenance. Pay your bills before they're due. (If you can't, call them before they call you.) Have that extra set of keys made now. Keep your tax materials separate and in order. In short, don't wait until you *have* to do something.

7) Balance #6 with prudence. Recognize what *doesn't* have to be done.

8) Ask yourself, "What annoys me the most?" Pet peeves may seem silly, but if they bug you, they'll crop up to cause you stress and sap your problem-solving strengths — strengths you'll need in a crisis. When you've identified the little problems, ask yourself what you can do about them. It's important to remember you always have options!

EXERCISES TO STRENGTHEN
YOUR CREATIVE POWERS FOR PROBLEM-SOLVING
AND STRENGTHEN YOUR ABILITY TO ADAPT

1) Catch yourself when you find yourself thinking there is only one way to do something. Resist the impulse to correct someone else's method. A weekend at your in-laws is a wonderful exercise.

2) Deviate from your routine. If you normally shower, take a bath. Take a different route to work. Don't eat lunch at noon unless you're hungry. Take a bus if you usually drive. Make something for dinner you've never tasted before. Change the rules of a game.

3) After watching a TV program or reading a novel, rewrite the ending in your mind. What would happen if the hero did this?_____

_____

_____

_____

   What other options did the characters have?_____

_____

_____

_____

4) In a friendly discussion of an issue with different viewpoints, set your opinion aside and argue for the opposite view.

5) Take a couple of kitchen or workshop gadgets and think up at least five new uses for them. A fork, for example, could be used to make decorative tracks on a cucumber, or trace intricate designs onto a frosted cake. Stand it up in a glass and it holds recipe cards in its tines. It's a garden tool, it's a drying rack for shoelaces. It's a vine support for drooping houseplants. It's a catapult for mashed potatoes. . . . You get the idea.

Item	Item
1._____	1._____
2._____	2._____
3._____	3._____
4._____	4._____
5._____	5._____

6) Play "what-if." What if you were stranded on a desert island? Fortunately your supply of C-rations washed ashore with you.
How do you open the cans? _____

Think up your own "what-ifs." _____

_____

_____

_____

_____

Chapter Seven

MOTIVATION

You will become as small as your controlling desire; as great as your dominant aspiration.

James Allen

One of the most crucial components of a Champion is motivation.

Over and over I have seen in my practice people whose lethargy makes it a wonder they even made it into my offices. "I just can't seem to get motivated," they sigh. "Nothing motivates me."

No wonder! They're looking for someone or something to act upon them, as if motivation were some sort of electrical juice that can be introduced into their systems.

Motivation is often misunderstood as some external force that compels us to action. Motivation is not external. It is internal, as James Allen states above. Its root word is "motive" which means an inner drive, impulse or intention. A motive is a *reason*, a *goal* which causes us to act in a certain way.

If you don't have a reason for doing something, you probably won't do it. There are exceptions for this — children under five, for example. They always claim they don't know why they colored on the bedspread. But that's another book.

Motivation is a noun, not a verb. The proliferation of "motivational experts" with their energetic electric delivery, pacing and gesticulating have unwittingly blurred the distinction between "motivation" and "motivate." Motivation is what motivates us. Period. I can't motivate you. Tapes and books can't motivate you. *Only your motives can motivate you.* If you do "get motivated" by this book, or by an evangelist's sermon, or by an inspirational seminar, it only *seems* like it. What has really happened is that something that was said touched upon one of your motives — a reason which was already inside of you.

Our motives are usually determined by our values. Your wife asks you if you think she's fat. (You think she is.) You respond by saying, "I think you're just right, honey." Your motive for fibbing was determined by your values. You value harmony more than you value honesty.

No one can "motivate" you any more than someone can "valuate" you. And unless you know what your values are, you have little on which to base your goals.

"Without a personal philosophy, a strong perception of who you are and what you stand for, you get buffeted around by every person, message, idea and event that comes down the pike," says David Mahoney in his book *Confessions of a Street-Smart Manager* (1988). These thoughts are as true now as they were over one hundred years ago, when John Stuart Mill said, "He who lets the world or his own portion of it, choose his plan of life for him, has no need of any faculty than the ape-like one of imitation."

Each day we busy ourselves about the business of so many things which do not reflect our values. After we have expended the best part of our time and energy on this business, we are left with only the dregs to cast at those matters which are *really* important to us.

Knowing what our values are provides tremendous freedom. By having a clear vision of what, precisely, is important to us, we are freed from all the extraneous demands on our time and energy on things which *do not matter*.

This irrational rationing of ourselves causes stress, because we are not comfortable with ourselves. We know that we are paddling someone else's canoe upstream instead of our own. We are expending time and energy on someone else's agenda, not ours.

As we have discussed, confidence is marked by an absence of stress. It is a circular sort of thing: lack of confidence is both a cause and an effect of stress. By zeroing in on your values you can make measurable headway in your upstream journey.

Not only will your stress level be reduced and your confidence level rise, the practical matter of time comes into play. With a finite amount of hours and energy at our disposal, it is clearly a waste to spend them on things that don't matter.

So decide what matters. Your values will determine almost everything else about you, and they are fundamental to each of the qualities of a CHAMPION.

Goals

If you don't have any, then you are simply a bystander or pawn, in pursuit of other people's goals.

As we discussed earlier in the book, adversity is anything that sets itself in the way of our goals. Consequently, a simple solution to adversity is not to have a goal. If you don't care where you end up, downstream will do just fine. You can simply let life carry you where it will. If you aren't moving forward, there can be no setback.

If we lacked even the basic motivation of survival, starvation would not be an adversity. Of course, few people are entirely devoid of goals. What separates the Champions from the people who don't make it, is the number, the degree, and the clarity of their goals.

Most of us do have goals beyond survival, but they are too vague, too nebulous, for them to be of any use to us. That is why clarity of motivation is so important. We must know precisely what we want in order to pursue it.

The lack of clarity in our motivation is responsible for a common ailment that the French term "ennui." We all know the feeling: a vague sense of dissatisfaction, an itch we can't scratch, a general feeling of discontent or listlessness. We want something but we don't know what. It is our body and our mind telling us that we have a purpose, a reason for being, but we haven't focused on it.

Mitzi Brown is a perfect example of this. Mitzi was the victim of a car accident that left her severely brain-damaged. To her doctors' and family's dismay, more than a month after the accident she awoke from her coma and opened her eyes. But there was no recognition in them. She was unaware of her surroundings, and she did not speak. She simply lay there. Her reason for being, her motives, were erased with her memory when a part of her brain was destroyed by the accident. Without these motives Mitzi was apathetic, lethargic, and was content to sit in her chair. Life held no purpose or promise.

Champions have focused on their purpose. They have a destination, therefore they have direction. They know that their thoughts and actions affect the direction in which they move.

The human need for purpose is very powerful. In Mitzi, it was powerful enough to create new neural pathways in her brain. Finding the way to conscious thought blocked by the debris of the brain damage, her subconscious thoughts charted a new course through the intricate maze of her mind. The reasons for Mitzi Brown's life fought their way to the surface. She gradually recognized her children, her husband, her cherished role as wife and mother. And with this recognition came direction.

"I wanted to learn everything I could," Mitzi says. "I wanted to please everyone." Especially her husband, Pat Brown. "I had to learn everything I could because I didn't want to lose him. I had such a crush on him!"

In many cases, Champions do not merely resume where they left off in the pursuit of their goals when adversity strikes. Often, the adversity itself presents the Champion with a new set of goals, a new direction.

As mentioned previously, after my divorce and being a student of life, I realized that I had focused much more on being a financial provider for my family rather than on my role as a husband and father. Like the many others who have overcome the pain of a setback, I learned from my mistakes and turned my energy into focusing on a new identity, with a new purpose. Along with my newly re-established role as a more compassionate and loving "daddy" to my two children, I also learned to appreciate the relationships with my friends, colleagues, and students more. I now spend more time with my children, not just time, but quality time. Very few moments go by when they are in my company that are not spent telling one of them that I love them or giving them a hug. Shortly after my divorce, I felt that I had discovered a new appreciation of people in general. I felt as if I had to find a way to share my feelings, opinions, and sympathetic ear to as many people as possible. By focusing my energy outward I found a path to reach out and try to touch as many people as possible. That has been by being a radio talk show host on a call in show every Sunday evening from 9:00 P.M. to midnight, on a 50,000 clear watt channel reaching people in over half of the United States. Every Sunday night my radio family and I sit for three hours and discuss the stresses and complexities of daily life. I have found my new relationship with my children and with my radio family to be the most rewarding feelings I have yet to experience, and they all came about by a change in my identity, purpose, and direction after my divorce.

"My priest told me that maybe God let me live because there was something I had not yet done," confides Mitzi. "Something I had not finished or something I would have to do in the future. I thought that was so nice of God, to give me a chance to finish." Mitzi's direction then shifted to the higher purpose she believed that God intended for her.

She incorporated her original focus of being a good wife and mother with her new goals: to fulfill what plan God had for her. She hesitates to say definitively what that plan might be, as if fulfilling it may signal the end of her purpose. "Maybe I lived because of the children," Mitzi speculates, wondering if the two girls she and Pat adopted may have been part of the plan. Regardless, the belief that her life held a definite purpose was one of the crucial points in Mitzi's recovery and in her ensuing years.

A temporary plunge into darkness, paralysis, or even death can profoundly shake a person's previous values and cause him to rethink his life when given a second chance.

Near-death experiences (NDE's) have been researched and analyzed by scientists in an effort to determine what, if anything, lies beyond this life. As a psychologist, I find the most intriguing result of the studies to be the almost universal sense of mission and purpose that emerge in these survivors. Regardless of what was really experienced during the NDE, the resulting changes made in the survivor's life are remarkable.

Kenneth Ring, Ph.D., author of *Heading Toward Omega*, found in studies of 111 NDE-ers that their lives had been radically transformed by the experience. The pattern of this transformation emerged in a greater appreciation of life, greater tolerance, compassion, higher self-esteem, less concern with material goods and status, and a heightened spirituality. Ring found that most exhibited a need to find a greater meaning for their lives. Simply stated, the experience caused a shifting of values and goals.

Being near-death is not the only catalyst to a new discovery of direction. Any sort of setback can cause the same kind of change.

John Howard Griffin came home from World War II blinded and an invalid. Living in darkness for over a decade, Griffin's sight was restored by surgery in a miracle that would change his life. In an irony not lost on the writer, Griffin's sight was restored not so much by the surgery as by his blindness. As a blind man, Griffin discovered that the color of a man's skin made no difference to him, even though he had spent his life as a racist. It was this insight, along with his regained eyesight, that prompted him to conduct the now-famous experiment of living as a black man, which he chronicled in his book *Black Like Me* (1961).

Teenager Ryan White, a hemophiliac who contracted the AIDS virus through a blood transfusion, turned his personal adversity into a crusade for other young victims. White caught the nation's attention in 1985 with his fight to attend public school in Kokomo, Indiana. As a public school student on the honor roll at Hamilton Heights, White continued to focus his energies on his cause to eradicate prejudice and discrimination against AIDS victims. Speaking to national conventions, before the TV cameras, and to audiences worldwide, Ryan's life had direction and meaning beyond his day-to-day survival. Ryan died in 1990 and for a young boy whose goals before his illness were likely no more ambitious than most boys his age, this new-found purpose had given him the secret with which to build the Champion within himself.

Two-thirds of the respondents to a Gallup Poll of 1500 prominent people listed in *Who's Who in America* indicate that they have had clear cut goals for themselves (Gallup, Gallup & Proctor, 1986). Again, the emphasis is on clear-cut. Clarity is very important.

Having a solid motive which outlines your direction diffuses the need or the penchant for excuses. We never excuse our efforts to attain something we think is important, and we don't look for excuses to get out of doing something we want to do. It's amazing how we can find the time and energy to do what pleases us. Because they have a goal which pleases them, Champions do not use their adversity as an excuse.

Texas Senator Bill Sarpalius never used his childhood as an excuse, although adversity was all he knew during his formative years. He lived with poverty, an absentee father and alcoholic mother, and polio which kept him out of school for two years.

Finally, he and his brothers, whose paper routes provided the sole family income, were sent to Boys Ranch, an institution in the Texas Panhandle. It was there that he decided he wanted to help others improve themselves, just as he then vowed to do.

"One of the big advantages of living in America is freedom of choice," he says, "I tell kids 'Dream your dreams and make them come true.'" Bill Sarpalius had a reason for becoming a success: to give back what he got as a youngster.

It makes sense to lock in your coordinates before you're under attack. The stress of adversity will likely throw off your thinking, and clear-cut goals and a clear purpose will be that much harder to attain.

We cannot achieve what we cannot dream. In the story to follow, meet a young marksman who summoned the motivation to rebuild his dream from an anguished nightmare.

MOTIVATION

Something to Think About and Do

He was twenty-seven years old and had set his sights on his goals — literally. The Rawlins, Wyoming, native was an expert marksman and his shooting career was right on target. By 1976 he had claimed the title of National High Power Champion-Marksman class, and he was just beginning.

Roger Withrow, whom you read about earlier as being an outstanding collegiate champion as a rifle marksman, was on the verge of worldwide recognition. He had a great track record in ROTC competitions along with other national titles.

The Pan American Games and the 1980 Olympics were within range, and he was lining them up in the crosshairs.

But that fall, Roger developed a painful herniated disc, and dropped out of school. The rehabilitation process would take some time — time Roger hadn't planned on — but the optimistic young man still had his targets locked in. He was the best in the nation, and now he was shooting for best in the world.

The set-back was an inconvenience, to be sure, but the intense young man with the wind-blown blond hair was convinced it was merely temporary. He would be back at Murray State for the next semester.

For a time, Roger's predictions of recovery were well-founded. He was steadily improving while working for his father's construction company back in Rawlins. His dad arranged for him to help out in ways that would not put stress on his back, and Roger was enjoying helping out and supervising. The seemingly endless stretches of open sky in Wyoming were a perfect backdrop for his shooting practice, and the secure, familiar feeling of being home was good therapy. He could feel the Olympic dream drawing closer to his grasp.

Then on May 7, 1979, all the days of Roger's rigorous preparation came undone. Roger Withrow's dreams came quite literally crashing down on him. Roger was out on a coal mining site, helping to supervise the construction of a load-out spur, a giant railroad track loop that would allow trains to turn around after unloading. A truck had arrived with a load of 20 foot by 3 foot corrugated steel pipes. Roger walked around behind the truck to show the workmen where to unload.

Then, the unthinkable happened. There was a rumbling, the unmistakable sound of metal against metal. The safety chain holding back the tons of steel was giving way.

"Look out!" someone shouted. But the realization was a split second too late.

"I dove head first to get under the truck," Roger recalled. "Unfortunately, I didn't dive hard enough or quick enough."

The first pipe came crashing down on Roger's legs with such force that he was flipped back out from under the truck, right into the path of the steel avalanche. Roger met the second assault while laying face up in the mud. Several tons of steel rolled over his body.

And then it stopped. The first tier of pipe had been unleashed, but the second tier remained secure. Roger Withrow lay dying in the mud.

"I couldn't breathe. Any time I tried to breathe, I couldn't exhale. I couldn't talk. The air was too valuable to talk. The truck driver and the other workers were too afraid to do anything. I remember looking them in the eye, trying to communicate . . . to tell them I couldn't breathe. There was an overwhelming feeling of panic."

Roger had a punctured lung. Deflated and compressed like a punctured balloon, his lung could not inflate and allow him to take in air. Every cell was starved for oxygen, and Roger felt himself losing consciousness.

"Slowly, everything started to go fuzzy. I remember thinking, 'I'm too young to die now. No, please, God — not now!' And then everything went black."

Inexplicably, after Roger had lost consciousness, he began coughing violently. His body wracked by the involuntary spasms, his friends and co-workers could only look on helplessly. And yet, Roger is certain that the coughing was God's answer to his desperate prayer.

Doctors later surmised that the violent coughing forced the air back into Roger's lungs, reinflating them so he could breathe again. Roger began to regain consciousness.

"My ribs and my chest were hurting bad. It was excruciating," he recalled. Doctors would later tell him that he had broken more than a dozen ribs. His back was broken, an irreparable tangle of nerve, muscle, and bone.

Roger could only feel the crushing pain in his torso. There was no pain in his legs. "I knew right then that I was a paraplegic, or worse. There was almost a mystical knowledge."

Roger recalls thinking about some of the friends he had grown up with. Joe Gonzales: relegated to a wheelchair since a car accident in high school. Kenny Roberts: a quadriplegic as a result of a diving accident. "I remember saying to myself, 'Look out, Joe, here I come. Kenny, move over.' There was this total acceptance that I was from that moment a paraplegic."

The local volunteer fire department arrived and loaded Roger in the ambulance. They drove him to the closest medical facility available — a little emergency center in town. The lone doctor knew Roger's condition was beyond the capacity of a facility designed to treat broken toes and cut fingers. He gave Roger an IV to stabilize him and instructed the ambulance drivers to get Roger to Casper, Wyoming, without delay. Roger's father walked in just at that moment. He saw his son lying there, and his face went ashen. Roger could only gaze silently at his stricken father, only too aware of the anguish he was causing. His father ran out to the truck, and sped off to meet the ambulance in Caspar.

The 127 mile drive to Caspar was tortuous. Scared and in tremendous pain, Roger had no choice but to endure the high-speed ride. When they arrived at the hospital, Roger's mother, father, brother, and sister-in-law were waiting.

Doctors wanted to operate immediately, but Roger's parents were not satisfied with what they were hearing. They wanted to bring in specialists, but the doctors would not agree.

Meanwhile, Roger's sister-in-law had been in touch with the Mayo Clinic. They advised that Roger be flown in immediately. Unconvinced that surgery without the specialists they had requested was in the best interests of their son, Mr. and Mrs. Withrow had Roger released.

On May 10, Roger was flown into Rochester, Minnesota, by air ambulance. For a year and a half, his home would be the sterile corridors of the Mayo Clinic. The familiar feel of gunmetal and wood in his hands was replaced by the stainless steel bars of hospital beds, and the smell of hot gun powder in his nostrils gave way to antiseptics and disinfectants.

The first of his more than thirty surgeries came only after seven days of exhaustive examination and diagnosis of Roger's condition. Before they could operate, doctors needed to know as much as they could about the extent of his injuries.

Finally, they went in. Surgeons fused vertebrae T-10 through L-1 in an effort to reconstruct his mangled spine. Despite the best efforts of the best doctors in the country, Roger's injuries were too extensive to repair. Upon awaking from surgery, doctors told Roger what he had known a week ago laying in the mud in Rawlins, Wyoming. He had lost the use of his legs.

Roger was a paraplegic. The strong, steady body of the marksman would no longer take the standing, kneeling, or prone postures required by international shooting competition regulations. Roger was paralyzed from the waist down. Three vertebrae were crushed, severing the electrical impulses from his brain to his legs.

In addition to the massive damage to his back and chest, his right ankle had been crushed, and the ligaments torn from his right knee. It took four screws to pin Roger's foot together.

"That was just the beginning," said Roger. "Those first surgeries were just to get started, to get me put back together. The rest were maintenance." In fact, Roger has had almost thirty-five surgeries since the accident, none of which could bring back the motor functions in his legs.

His dream of bringing home the gold for the United States in the 1980 Olympics had been crushed along with his body. The skill and the talent that had been his obsession were now merely memories to be placed on the mantle with his hundreds of trophies and plaques.

The agonizing months of recuperation and rehabilitation at the Mayo Clinic pushed Roger to his limits. In severe pain, Roger relied on Demerol, Valium, and morphine to get him through each excruciating day. Dependent upon other people for his physical needs, he slowly found himself losing further control as he began to slip into a dependence upon the pharmaceutical drugs.

When the Valium started to give him headaches, Roger was prescribed marijuana as a clinical alternative to the tranquilizer. He was now mixing drugs and grass.

"I became a 'head.' Of course, I wasn't the only one. There were plenty of others like me up there. We used to sit around and smoke grass while looking out the window over Rochester."

The initial acceptance of his fate that day of the accident began to change. Gone was the man who had told Joe Gonzales and Kenny Roberts to move over. The stoic who had decided he would be the best paraplegic that ever pushed a wheelchair was sinking into a deep depression.

"I was very depressed. It was a very low period in my life," said Roger. "I began to feel sorry for myself. I kept asking 'Why me?' Right after the accident I was just so glad to be alive, I could only think about how great I was going to handle things. But then I lost perspective."

Roger continued in his gentle, soft-spoken manner. "I was really bummed out. Everything got to me. The wheelchair. The loss of my legs. The bowel care, bladder training . . . a grown man wetting his pants is very embarrassing and humiliating. So I was really down. My attitude had really regressed. Then I would feel guilty for feeling sorry for myself when I should have been grateful for being alive. So I'd get even more depressed."

Roger dwelled on the things he couldn't do. His shooting career, which was and had been his sole direction for so long, was gone. He brooded over a future that held no children for him, a devastating blow to a man who envisioned himself with many children. At twenty-seven years old, he was a man with nothing to live for.

Finally, both Roger and his doctors knew that if Roger was going to make any progress, something drastic had to happen. Roger's doctor recommended six weeks in the open psychiatric unit.

Roger was not at all sure, nor was his family. "The most difficult thing to cope with was being labeled crazy," Roger reflects. "The first two weeks were hell. The labeling was internal, of course. I was the one who was calling myself crazy."

Roger was no stranger to adversity. His high-school sweetheart, with whom he was deeply in love, had committed suicide. Roger found the body. When he was six, he lost his grandmother to cancer, and his grandfather, inconsolable after the loss of his wife, had also committed suicide.

Somehow the young man, saddled with so much mental anguish at such a young age, had survived. And now he would have to summon the courage to do it again, only this time the stakes were that much higher. The tragic set-back of the accident which forever altered Roger's physical being was now threatening his very existence. Would he be just one more wheelchair by the window, passing the hours of his life in silent resignation?

Those six weeks in the psychiatric unit challenged every fiber of his being, but he emerged with a strong determination to shake his dependency on drugs and self-pity. He may not ever walk again, but he swore that that would be his only limitation.

There was something inside of Roger Withrow that wasn't destroyed by the crushing force of a truckload of steel. Something inside him that allowed him to see possibilities, and beyond that, to make those possibilities a reality. Roger knew this wasn't to be the end of his magnificent shooting career.

In 1982, Roger went to the Pan American Games he had dreamed of. He had just never dreamed they would be the VII Pan Am Wheelchair Games in Halifax, Nova Scotia. There he set the record for both Air Pistol and Prone Air Rifle events. In that same year, Roger pioneered the Air Gun Sports section for the National Wheelchair Athletic Association and served as its chairman through 1985.

As the first athlete to represent the United States in the shooting events of the International Wheelchair Games, he grabbed fourteen gold medals, eleven silver medals, and two bronze medals from 1982 to 1987. He amassed twelve gold medals, and one silver in several different shooting events in his three appearances at the National Wheelchair Games.

Next stop — the VII World Paralympics in the United Kingdom. There Roger racked up a near perfect score of 397 out of a possible 400 in the prone Air Rifle Competition to grab a world title. The record held for two years when it was finally broken with an incredible score of 398 of 400. But Roger was not disappointed. It was he who had broken his previous record.

Roger was not content to be merely the best that he could be; he was determined to pave the way for other athletes as well. During his term as chairperson of the National Wheelchair Shooting Federation, Roger pioneered the movement to increase the visibility of the sport for wheelchair athletes, and to gain the same status enjoyed by able-bodied participants in shooting events. In 1985, he became the first resident wheelchair athlete at the U.S. Olympic Training Camp in Colorado Springs, where he still resides today.

The events keep coming, and Roger keeps winning, continually finding records to break. In 1986, at the Pan American Wheelchair Games in Puerto Rico, he set a Pan Am record for number of medals won by a single athlete. Then it was off to Australia and the United Kingdom in 1987, where he continued to bring home the gold and set world records.

Having accomplished what for many is a lifetime of goals in just the few short years since recovering from his accident, what mountains are there left to climb? For Roger, the prospect of chipping away at the obstacles separating the disabled and the able-bodied is his next challenge. Discouraged with the relative lack of world class competition in events slated for disabled athletes, Roger would like to see a new category created in the Olympics. Rather than a separate Olympics — the Paralympics — Roger sees a disabled category within the Olympics itself which would address the inevitability of the chair. Opponents of his views point out that the chair could provide unequitable advantage in steadying the athlete.

Regardless, Roger went to Seoul, as a member of the United States Sports Disabled Team.

His involvement in sports extends beyond the target range. He rations his energy to leave enough for the life he is building for the time when he will no longer compete. Coaching and sports medicine are natural progressions for the intense young man who throughout his life has been able to draw a bead on his target and hit it dead center.

What is it about Roger that enables him to so consistently and continuously pursue his goal despite his set-backs? What qualities does Roger possess that allow him to see not what might have been but what can be? What makes Roger paddle upstream?

EXERCISES ONE CAN USE TO COMBAT ADVERSITY

1) Recall a recent setback within the last few years. Think of what was important to you *before* the setback. Try to ignore the current circumstance. What was your goal, your purpose then? _____

_____

_____

_____

2) Is this goal still important to you now?_____
If not, why?_____

_____

_____

If not, discard it. If it is still important, why is it important? (Do not think about plausibility at this point.)_____

_____

_____

3) If it is still important to you, retain it, clarify it, and make it specific. If your adversity has made your goal implausible, hang on to it anyway.

4) If your goal is no longer important to you, or if you were unable to pinpoint your goals or purpose in your life before the setback, now is the time to focus. Resist the impulse to give as your goal "to get through this." You need a *destination*. "Getting through it" is merely a route. You will now see the direction you are going.

5) Now, set short-term goals. These are the landmarks along the river, and they will be the signposts that will indicate that you are making progress. This is the "getting through it" part.

_____

_____

Chapter Eight

PERSPECTIVE

It is our attitude at the beginning of a difficult undertaking which, more than anything else, will determine its successful outcome.

William James

When you face the fact of your own mortality, you must also face the facts of what you have done with your life. It is a painful lesson and a difficult journey, but I am personally grateful that I was made to travel this path at an early age. For I have learned much about myself, much about what I want out of life, and much about how precious life and people are. It is our relationships with others, especially those whom we love, that give the fullest meaning to life.

Following my cancer surgery, my father, mother, sister, and I all realized how distant we had become from one another emotionally. Through much determination on all of our parts we worked hard to make the bonds between us stronger. I realized how precious life was, and their standing by me in this time of great difficulty really brought out in me how important one's family is. My father died seven years after my illness, however, during those seven years we truly learned how to love one another. I truly loved my father for he is the man who taught me how to come back from adversity for he himself had many setbacks in his life that he had to overcome.

A charming woman I know who has survived her cancer for nine years tells me how the diagnosis changed her life. "I used to get all bent out of shape over the little things which I now know were meaningless," she says. "I would fuss and fume over a thoughtless comment or an overlooked birthday. Now I can say 'Who cares?' and mean it. Life is too important to waste on such trivia!"

Adversity has a way of providing us with a new perspective on life which we may otherwise never have gotten and, as James says above, this new attitude will determine how successful we will be in overcoming our setbacks. Rabbi Alexander Schindler, President of the Union of American Hebrew Congregations, gained a new perspective following a severe heart attack and several days of intensive care. In his commencement address to the University of South Carolina in 1987, Rabbi Schindler shared his new-found insight. "Life's gifts are precious, but we are too heedless of them," he says. "We must seek a wider perspective, viewing our lives as though through windows that open on eternity. Once we do that, we realize that though our lives are finite, our deeds on Earth weave a timeless pattern."

What Schindler said so eloquently goes to the heart of perspective. *Webster's Dictionary* (1988) defines perspective as the "relationship or proportion of the parts of a whole, regarded from a particular standpoint or point of time." The standpoint Schindler suggests is through "windows that open on eternity."

Such a vantage point is not easily taken. Sometimes the only way we can ever achieve another point of view is to get knocked off our comfortable roost. We are forced to look at things from a new perspective — from the bottom up.

When I was first diagnosed with cancer, my viewpoint toppled from the lofty perch of academia to the hard pavement of mortality. Looking at life from the bottom up was a new perspective, one which I would not have chosen, but nevertheless have come to value. In an odd way, I am thankful for it. Had I not been forced into a position of looking up, I would never have seen the stars. Henry Kaiser said he always viewed problems as "opportunities in work clothes."

Another person for whom life's circumstance afforded a new perspective was James Gardner, the former mayor of Shreveport, Louisiana. Gardner, Vice President of Southwestern Electric Power Company, was widowed at age fifty-two, and the following year he underwent open heart surgery. "I have discovered an ability to savor life in a manner that I had not known prior to adversity," he said in a commencement address to the Class of '76, Louisiana State University at Shreveport. "Deep pain can awaken your sensitivity to life."

This heightened awareness and acuity of insight is both a gift to, and a characteristic of, a Champion.

Significant losses often serve as turning points in individuals' lives and lead to new perspectives on the meaning of what is important in life. Indeed, suffering appears to be a necessary ingredient in integrating loss into a life plan that is full of joy, wonder, and appreciation.

Adversity's hand touches us and tilts our heads just so . . . until we are able to get a glimpse of promise. Just as we cannot see the rainbow if the light is not refracted to our eye, the deeper joys of life are not evident without the perspective of loss.

Revelations, or shifts of viewpoint, generally occur as a result of something bad or unpleasant which happens. Suffering may be necessary in order to get a true perspective on the meaning of life. While those who are blessed with health, comfort, and happiness are not necessarily excluded from the ranks of those with perspective, it is true that we hear fewer stories of people who have gained new meaning in life, and a renewed sense of sensitivity to life from a clean bill of health or a job promotion. Both experiences would be intensified, however, against the backdrop of previous adversity in health or in finances.

Pain and suffering, then, is the horizon line on the canvas, and our life's picture is painted in the correct perspective, always using the horizon line to determine where to place life's events and values.

For some, perspective arrives suddenly, like an awakening. "I was at my friend's mother's funeral," said an acquaintance of mine. "It was very depressing, very sad. I didn't know her well, so I wasn't really affected by her death. I was affected by her family. My friend was completely torn up, crying, and terribly distraught. I tried to comfort him—it wasn't like him to be so emotional. Finally he turned his tear-stained face to me. 'I hadn't seen Mom for over a year,' he wept. 'And the last words she heard from me were 'go to hell.'" My friend's perspective changed that instant. ("I left the funeral home, stopped by the florist, and went to see my own mother.") Jim has done this every Thursday since the funeral almost a dozen years ago.

Sometimes perspective is achieved only with brutal honesty with oneself. Only then can we come to see the true picture, and begin to change it.

The mother of an infant born with a rare abnormality told me of her pain and grief for her baby who would never be like other children. "For the first few months I was so angry," she said. "Until I realized that what I was experiencing was really shame—shame that I had produced something so imperfect. I wasn't grieving for her, I was grieving for me!"

Once this young mother had come to grips with why she was grieving, she could begin to take control of her feelings and effect change.

"All this self-pity wasn't going to do a thing for my daughter," she realized. "So I quit looking for ways to help me cope and started looking for ways to prepare her to cope."

We can see from the stories mentioned above how perspective can be received, earned, or learned. To receive it, we must be open to it, and to be earned or learned we must be willing to work for it was well as to be open to it. Adversity and suffering alone do not guarantee a good perspective. It is this openness we need to cultivate if we are to avail ourselves of the riches of perspective.

A sensitivity to the joys and meaning of life are not the only perspective we can have. Perspective affords us a point of view, and while studies and experience indicate that suffering is necessary to achieve a higher plane of meaning for our lives, we can gain perspective from the less tragic stressors of life as well.

As with the profound perspective such as might be gained from a near-death experience or the loss of a child, a good, healthy perspective on life can be a potent immunization against the slings and arrows of life. Like most immunizations, you have to be exposed to the disease to develop the immunity.

Katy tells how growing up in an alcoholic family provided the perspective which helps her in her life today. "I belong to an ACOA group (Adult Children Of Alcoholics) which got me to see my co-dependent behavior, which I've really worked on overcoming. But I don't see co-dependency as all bad. My constant need to please and to take responsibility is really an asset in many ways. I work in a service industry where a lot of people have problems dealing with the public, always being smiley and helpful. For me, it's a breeze!" she says. "I also feel that I appreciate my own independence more, and I really value my happiness."

This perspective is not merely optimism; it is the same reality which had Katy feeling angry, hurt and confused before. But a new point of view of both herself and her situation allowed her to see the same things differently. This change of viewpoint has been discussed in research as well. Garmezy (1985) called upon Rachman's concept of "learned helpfulness" (similar to learned helplessness discussed in the chapter on Confidence) to describe the heightened morale and acquisition of problem-solving skills in some children in stressed environments. I believe that the children who did emerge with positive resources did so because of a point of view not held by the less resilient children.

Point of view can be affected by many factors, one of the most popular and time-honored being the "count your blessings factor." While it may seem quaint and trite — particularly in a society where we are inundated with the "me first" philosophy — it really does work.

Way back in the fourth century B.C., Democritus of Abdera offered this sage advice: "You should contemplate the lives of those who suffer hardship, and vividly bring to mind their sufferings so that your own present situation may appear to you important and to be envied, and so that it may no longer be your portion to suffer torture in your soul by your longing for more."

Through history, we find more such exhortations. Such diverse personalities as Danté, Chaucer, and Queen Elizabeth have drawn courage and comfort from the writings of sixth century philosopher Boethius. In his essay "Every Man Has His Cross," Boethius offers the following:

"Thou art thinking now, for instance, that thou art very unhappy, and yet I know that many a man would fancy himself raised up to heaven if he had any part of the happiness which is still remaining to thee."

This is still good advice, and shows up repeatedly in Champions who prevail over adversity. We can gain a portion of the perspective that is usually reserved for those who suffer tragedy themselves when we vicariously experience their pain. We emerge, however temporarily, with a finer appreciation for our own lives.

Perspective also rids us of the "someday I'll." Someday I'll take that trip or someday I'll have time to spend at home with the kids is a day that just may never come. If we are always looking for happiness in something someday, we miss it right under our noses.

When Massachusetts Senator Paul Tsongas was diagnosed with lymphoma, in 1983, he resigned his Senate seat in order to spend time with his family, time which he had never seemed to have enough of. The insight he gained from confronting his own mortality convinces him he did the right thing. "Life is a search for balance," says Tsongas, "for a way to bring the scales back to center. Every day I know the fragility of my health, and my mortality. But my real worry is that I will lose my current sense of values and perspective as the nightmare of October 1983 fades from memory. If I remain symptom-free, will I go back to the mind-set I had before . . . ? I pray not. I want always to feel as I do now" (Tsongas, 1984).

The proper perspective can do wonders to dispel that philosophy, and often times it's as a result of some misfortune that jerks our heads around and makes us look at someday from a different viewpoint. How often have you succumbed to the "Someday I'll" philosophy? The grieving son at his mother's funeral no doubt had some vague thought about reconciling with his mother — someday. Jim got his head jerked around that day and was cured of his "Someday I'll" philosophy.

As previously mentioned, after my cancer surgery I gained a new perspective on the quality of life and relationships, most especially to the relationship with my family, which grew stronger after my bout with this potentially fatal illness. However, I was forced to go through something far more tragic several years after my surgery — the death of my marriage. Like a Champion, that too caused me to rethink and learn from life, gaining a new perspective towards my relationships with others, especially my two children.

Perspective given to us in times of adversity is available for our use in later troubles. A healthy dose of perspective always puts us at the right vantage point from which we can see a problem for what it really is and act accordingly.

Walter Cronkite suffered a blow to his self-esteem when he was dismissed by CBS from his position as anchorman of the 1964 Democratic National Convention. He kept this in perspective by recognizing that it was the network's prerogative to select another anchorman.

"It was their candy store," he said. His ability to put things in their perspective was undoubtedly a factor in CBS' decision to reinstate him. Such a perspective of reality is not always pleasant, but it is always the most instrumental in successful coping techniques among Champions.

Another angle from which we can look through the lens at life is upside down. Sometimes life isn't ordered precisely the way we want it. Instead of trying to make sense out of it, many people choose to be amused by its contradictions, and in doing so, diminish their problem.

"Humor is the universal salve," says Francine Klagsbrun, "easing tensions and marriage fatigue. If you can laugh about it, you know it will be all right."

Harpo Marx, "speaking" through Rowland Barber in *Harpo Speaks!*, reflects on the power of the humorous perspective. "Dad fielded gripes by reducing tragedy to absurdity. Soon you were laughing at yourself, and your problem faded away. He was a born healer."

The humorous perspective pops up repeatedly with Champions over adversity. It may seem strange to be talking about humor in some particularly tragic cases. What after all, can be even remotely amusing about pain, death, or suffering?

It is precisely that incongruity that may provide the answer. One definition of humor is the ability to perceive or appreciate that which is funny, amusing or ludicrous. It is the ability to recognize that which is inconsistent with reason or order, a 'What's wrong with this picture?' sort of mentality.

Our English word "humor" is taken from the Latin word "umor" which means moist or wet. Its English meaning was originally any of the four fluids formerly considered responsible for one's health and disposition. Hence, the usage of humor to describe one's mood: "He's in good humor today." The formulators of the language perhaps intuitively knew what scientists are just recently quantifying in research and clinical studies: Our moods can create physical effects in our bodies.

Hospitals are taking this theory that humor can have therapeutic effects and using it to assist in the treatment of patients for whom traditional methods are exhausted. Old Laurel and Hardy movies, for example, have been shown in cancer wards. "Laughter is the best medicine" is an old axiom now being legitimized by medical science. The practice of forbidding children to visit relatives in hospital rooms is now largely by the wayside, primarily because of the good cheer the children bring to the patients. The benefits of such therapy far outweigh the possible risk of children spreading germs, as was the thinking not so long ago.

Some researchers put forth convincing and encouraging evidence that the physical act of laughter produces endorphins, the body's own pain killing chemicals. Norman Cousins is a firm believer in laughter as a healer, and his book, *Anatomy of an Illness* (1979), chronicles his recovery from a serious collagen disease with his own prescription of massive doses of laughter and vitamin C. He bet his life on his theory, and he won.

At any rate, levity is becoming serious business in the health business, and for good reason. Research continues to provide exciting studies in that regard. While researchers do not promise cures for disease, many do predict that the likelihood of catching something is diminished with the perspective of humor.

This humorous perspective has been repeatedly theorized to be a modifier of stress, and the studies done on their behalf tend to bear them out. But the real research giants who prove the theory are the Champions, who with an incredible sense of cheer, make their pain easier to bear for themselves and those who must watch them suffer.

Who will ever forget the courageous story of James Brady? When John

Hinckley, Jr. squeezed off six bullets in the direction of President Ronald Reagan, one of them forever altered the life of Jim Brady. Brady, Reagan's Press Secretary, took a bullet in the head. Defying the odds, Brady did not die, nor was he a "vegetable" as so many feared. His left side almost completely paralyzed, James Brady fought back and learned to talk again, and much of what he said was funny.

Even before he regained speech, his humor was evident. "He was deliberately being funny," observed his therapist, Cathy Wynne. She described how Brady responded to a request that he stick out his tongue. He performed a "schtick" for his rapt audience, where he slapped the back of his head to pop the tongue out, and steered his tongue in all directions by pulling on the appropriate ear.

During his entire ordeal, Brady maintained his good humor. He continually joked with doctors and friends, and it served to lighten both his load and that of his family. The good humor was also an indicator that Brady's mind was working, and his perspective was healthy too. When a serious fever enveloped him and doctors feared a lethal connection with the brain injury, discovering that it was pneumonia was a blessed relief. The irony was not lost on Brady. "Whoopee, have you heard the good news?" says Brady. "I'm not sick. I've only got pneumonia."

His ability to perceive incongruity and derive amusement from it is characteristic of Champions, including former President Reagan, who is known for his wit. His comment to his wife Nancy, following the attempted assassination which downed his Press Secretary, was, "Honey, I forgot to duck." While a nation sat stunned and shocked, the two victims were making light of their situation!

A marriage therapist suggests that humor be used as a communication tool. Annette Goodheart, Ph.D., a psyshotherapist from Santa Barbara, California, suggests that "We are happy because we laugh, not the other way around." She advises her married clients to actively cultivate their sense of humor in tense situations. She asks them to agree to a key word or phrase which will elicit the memory of a funny incident. Then, when a tense situation arises, one of the partners will use that word or phrase.

"One couple remembered the time they made love outdoors—and the lawn chair folded up on them! They chose the words 'lawn chair' and agreed that whenever one of them invoked that phrase, their argument would stop,"

Goodheart says. "It always made them laugh and broke the tension to help them resolve the problem."

It will not only be all right, suggest other studies, it will be better. People with a sense of humor tend to be more creative and problem-solving oriented. One Israeli experiment involved having 141 tenth graders listen to a recording of a popular comedian. An equal number of students served as the control group and did not hear the recording. Both groups then took a standard creativity test. The students who listened to the comedy routine fared significantly better than the control group. These results suggest that since humor can point out the ambiguity of situations, it trains us to see things from a new and unexpected angle. This has promising application for those of us who aspire to cultivate the qualities of Champions. As we saw in the chapter on Adaptability, creative ways of looking at things are the mark of an adaptive style.

Perhaps Perspective is that ancient quality called wisdom. We call a person wise when he tells us something we know to be true, yet we never really thought about it like that before. Perhaps he sees things in perspective, from an angle we have never taken before. Perhaps he, too, has looked at life from the bottom up.

Think of a white sheet of paper with a black spot in the center. When you describe it to someone else, do you focus on the spot or the expanse of the white paper? It's all in one's perspective.

PERSPECTIVE

Something to Think About and Do

Karen M. is forty years old and a successful marketing executive in a large Midwestern city. Her talent in marketing and promotions appears to be a natural product of her strength and savvy. She tackles projects with seemingly bound- less energy, and she has a reputation for getting things done. Softspoken and self- confident, she is a lady in control.

To the casual onlooker, this attractive, poised woman's experience with adversity could have only occurred on paper, where success is determined monetarily. But for Karen, the corporate jungle is a trek through Busch Gardens compared to the harrowing journey she had already survived.

"My first recollection of my father molesting me is when I was five years old. He pulled me out of the bathtub and set me on his lap. . . ."

The tastefully decorated condo is full of self-help books, tapes, and magazines. A Sealpoint Siamese cat sits on the hall table as if placed there by an interior designer to accent the Oriental decor. The picture is one of calm and serenity. Karen gently strokes the baby cockatoo perched on her shoulder.

"Of course, that's my first recollection. I'm certain it had happened before. I remember watching my father climb into my sister's crib one time. So I'm sure I was still in diapers the first time."

Karen describes the monstrous details of the increasingly frequent moles- tations. The chronology of the events is muddled, and years overlap one another. One minute she is remembering events that took place when she was six, and the memory blends into an attack by her father when she was twelve. Fortu- nately, there is much that she has forgotten.

"You have to understand that I lived in denial for more than thirty years. What I had lived through as a child was too horrible to think about. So I didn't really say to myself 'I was molested by my father' until many, many years later. It was slowly revealed to me. I remember watching Charlie's Angels, and there were a bunch of girls mixed up in a porno ring. Tears started rolling down my face when I realized that I understood they were incest victims because that's what I was."

Until ten years ago, Karen had blocked out much of her childhood. The ghastly discovery of the secret she was keeping from herself revealed a childhood of torment and fear. She discovered an aching loneliness and a profound sadness in those recesses of her memory she had so long ago locked away. There was so much pain, and so much anger.

For most people, childhood is a time and place of safety from all that is hurtful, scary, or lonely. The adults in a child's world are trusted protectors, providing a safe haven from fears real or imagined. But for Karen, the bogeymen and monsters did not just live in her imagination. They lived in her house with her, and they were all too real.

As a young child, Karen could only know that which she observed and experienced. But even though her frame of reference did not include a normal healthy relationship with her parents, as a young child Karen instinctively knew that something felt very wrong, and she was terrified of her father.

Her young mind longed for answers to questions that she was not even capable of posing. A child yearning for love and acceptance, her thoughts mirrored the perversity in her life.

"My father was a cold, unemotional man. Of course, as a child, you want more than anything to please your parents and to get some sort of positive response from them. So you grab at any kind of straw to prove to yourself that you are loved."

Karen recalls how this basic need twisted her into a depraved sort of mindset. "My older brother was in the bathtub with me that one time when my father pulled me out. He reached in and chose me over my brother. I remember feeling pleased that I had been favored over my brother," she says. "I had wanted so desperately to be loved, to have some sort of attention from my father, somehow I was able to twist this horror around until it became something positive for me."

The incestuous cancer grew and spread. Karen recalls how the perversity pervaded the family. "That time in the bathroom, the three of us were in the bathroom together. My brother, my father, and me. My brother watched. He was almost seven."

Even at seven years old, her brother watched and learned. His father sent him a message that day in the bathroom, a terrifying message he would file away in his young mind and retrieve several years later.

"My brother learned that it was OK to do that to another person. Not too many years later, my brother raped me. I don't remember the details, whether there was an actual ejaculation or not, but there was rape. For a very long time I had no recollection of this. When I was thirteen, he raped me again. That's my next recollection, although I'm sure that there were other instances of molestation. By that time, with the history of my father, I was already a victim, and I was an easy target. I did what I was told."

Karen opened a letter on the table: "To a Sweet Daughter On Her Birthday." It was from her mother.

"My mother? She always looked the other way. Her survival was denial. To this day she denies. If the evidence was too obvious to ignore, she'd blame me. Two years ago I finally told her about my brother. She said, 'How can you say such awful things about your brother?

"It wasn't just me. He raped my sister too. We never talked about it until recently. My brother got increasingly violent, and started reading pornographic magazines. He'd tie us up and put things inside of us. . . .'"

Karen recounts her story with an eerie matter-of-factness. "When I was ten, I was walking home from playing ice hockey on the creek. One of my brother's friends approached me and asked if he could do to me what my brother had been doing. I was devastated, humiliated. He had told everyone. It was bad enough what was happening, but to have everyone know. . . . I felt such betrayal. Because of it, I never hung around with anyone from my school again."

Karen eventually summoned the strength to say no to her brother. "When I told him he would never touch me again," she recalls, "I did so out of fear of pregnancy, not out of any sense of self-esteem. I had no self-esteem, so I was unworthy to say no to him for all those years." It was only when she realized that she could conceive that she had a reason to deny him. "Up until then, I had no choice in the matter . . . and he did leave me alone, but not my sister. I was thirteen then."

Karen had mustered enough courage to stop her brother, but was unable to do the same with her father. The powerful control he wielded over Karen was too strong. She was there to do his bidding.

Karen remembers the sleepless nights, listening in cowering fear for the dreaded footsteps. She slept on the floor against the wall until her father bought her a trundle bed. She knew it was to make her more accessible.

Finally, she could take no more. She was fifteen years old, and she told her father that she would not submit any longer. If her forced her, she would leave.

"When I finally stood up to my father, he found ways to punish me, to make a show of his control. I had saved up to buy a drum so I could play in the band. It was the only school activity I had ever been in. It was so important to me. He took it from me. He told me I would never play in the band. To this day I have not picked up a musical instrument."

Claudia Black's *Adult Children Of Alcoholics* sits on the coffee table. "My parents were both alcoholics. Both my mother's parents were alcoholics too. So I cooked and cleaned and kept the family running from the time I was seven. I have no pleasant memories of mealtime. My father would come home and there would be a blitzkrieg in the kitchen. In addition to living in fear of the molestings, I was terrified of the screaming and the scenes. There was absolutely no love in that house. And yet I felt that by being good or by doing better, I could somehow make us a family."

The nightmarish childhood was made even more difficult by an undiagnosed learning disability. The cruel whisperings of unthinkable rumors about the young girl were combined with taunts and jeers for her backwardness.

"My self-esteem was so low. Not only did I have the incest and the alcoholism dragging me down, I felt stupid, too. I wrote things backwards and wore my shoes on the wrong feet. School was very hard, and very embarrassing for me. At that time, of course, I didn't know I had dyslexia. I learned that about twelve years ago. But you can imagine where my self-esteem was all that time. Maybe that's part of the reason I felt helpless to change my situation.

"I was stupid, and my father was so smart. He was a genius, actually. He was heavily into precision, measurements, that sort of thing. And I couldn't even get my shoes on the right feet!"

Karen recalls her first attempts at normal relationships after she had broken from the grip of her father's sexual tyranny. "I thought I was healing. I had gotten baptized in a Christian church, and the immersion in the water was a powerful cleansing for me. I felt that all the impurities had been washed away. I began seeing a boy. I really liked him, and after I began to trust someone for the first time in my life, I told him what was happening at home. Obviously, I had misread him completely, and his whole attitude toward me changed. Apparently he felt that I was a woman of experience, and how can you soil someone who's already soiled? So he raped me.

"I was devastated. I headed back into a tailspin. I sunk into deep depression and carried a death wish. I wasn't suicidal, but I had a death wish. I didn't eat, and I got down to about seventy-five pounds. I cut off all of my hair. I don't know why . . . maybe so I would just not be me anymore when I looked in the mirror.

"Finally, I got involved with another boy, and we dated for five years. No sex. And I thought this must be a good relationship because there was no sex. I didn't realize that there should be emotional paybacks. In looking back, I realize there was no warmth or love there either. He was gone one summer, so I began seeing another boy. I got pregnant by him. I knew if he found out, he'd make me have an abortion, so I ran away to Las Vegas with another boy I had known in high school. He knew I was carrying another man's child. But he wanted to marry me anyway. And I thought this was wonderful, so we got married."

Karen felt that she had finally escaped from the tormented life she had known. More than anything she wanted to be a wife and mother and to love and to be loved. She just knew that she had broken free.

Unfortunately, as Karen was growing up, she never learned what it was like to be loved, and consequently, poor imitations were often passed off as the real thing. In addition, her extremely low self-image and the masses of scar tissue surrounding her emotions left her ill-equipped to either accept love or to give love. She did not see the pattern of destructive behavior in her new husband until it became all too apparent. "He had an abusive history which, of course, I didn't recognize," Karen says. "He was an alcoholic and he was messed up from Viet Nam. Three years later he left me."

Three years of her life reduced to four sentences. Karen sees little point in elaborating, since for her, it was all just a sordid repetition of the life she had left behind.

Karen continues her story in the detached manner of someone relating the details of a book she had read. "I was back at my parents with a three-year-old son. I stayed there three weeks, then got a basement apartment. We had two cups, one plate, a few pieces of silverware, and a crib. I got a job bartending. I went through a very, very black period."

Conditioned to a life of use, abuse, and abandonment, Karen herself perpetuated the cycle. She embarked on a life-course of self-destruction.

"I became very promiscuous," she says. "I couldn't even count how many men I was with. Drive-through woman — Get a burger and get laid. I was a hot number. Push-up bra, hot pants . . . this was the image that had been given to me by my father and brother. I became pregnant by one of the men I had been seeing, and he and I decided to marry. I didn't marry because of the baby or because of love. I finally got married to control my promiscuity.

"For a while it was working. This was the best I had ever known. He was sixteen years older than I was. I guess I was looking for the father I never had. I don't know. At any rate, I thought everything would be all right now that I had a real family. That's all I ever wanted."

In the meantime, Karen's father had died. He had been in a sanitarium since shortly after she had first left home. His diabetes was out of control, mostly because of the drinking.

"He was having all kinds of delusions in his last years . . . he believed he invented the match. He would throw a piece of paper against the wall and perform all sorts of calculations on it. He died lonely and alone at the age of sixty. I thought I would be euphoric, but I wasn't. He had died without giving me what I needed . . . a father. He never apologized, never said he was sorry."

For the first time Karen's voice begins to quaver, and her clear blue eyes mist over. "You never stop wanting them to acknowledge the damage they've done . . . to say they're sorry."

After her father's death, Karen was sorting out the pieces of her life and struggling with her marriage. She was making progress. It was all behind her and she tried hard to look toward the future. The road was inevitably rocky. Given the distorted perceptions Karen had formed of life and of love, creating a happy, healthy family was a Herculean task. While marred with difficulties of intimacy and trust, Karen's marriage was better than anything she had ever known. She believed she was going to make it. And then one day, her world caved in.

"I remember the day I received a phone call from my daughter's counselor. She was in counseling to deal with her learning disability, the same one I had. I remember being angry because they wouldn't tell me what it was about, just that they insisted I come right down and meet with them. I was met by three police officers with badges. My daughter had revealed to her counselor that she had been molested by her grandfather. My mother's second husband."

The incestuous cancer was not in remission. After her husband's death, Karen's mother repeated her pattern of self-destructive behavior and started the cycle anew.

"I was completely devastated. I was hysterical and screaming, and the feeling of guilt was enormous. I had taught my daughter 'good-touch, bad-touch' when she was eight, but it had been too late. She was seven years old the first time it happened. How could I have allowed that to happen? I asked myself. How could I have done this to my own daughter?" Karen said, remembering her feelings. "There was enormous guilt. Knowing what I did about my mother's denial, how could I have let my daughter be alone with that man?"

Karen called her mother and told her about the molestations. Karen's mother admitted she had had some suspicions, and even showed Karen she had written down the things she had seen him doing. But when it came time for the court hearing, she denied everything, even the existence of the notebook.

"The deep, dark closet that I had kept shut for so many years had opened and everything fell out on me. I was back in a tailspin, and everything was falling apart. That was the end of our marriage. Paul had been having a hard enough time coping with me and my difficulties with intimacy, but now I was coming undone again. I guess I could have accepted his lack of support for me, but I wouldn't accept him turning his back on my daughter."

Karen's detached manner dissolves when she speaks about her children, and the anger is apparent. A mother lion with her cubs, one senses the reserves of strength she is able to summon up.

"The hearings and the trials ripped apart this family. It ripped apart my sisters and brothers and my mother and destroyed what little family there was. So, there I was again, without the only thing I had ever really wanted — a real family."

The years of physical and emotional trauma emerged in Karen's body as a disease called fibromiralgia, a muscle disorder. Simply stated, her body rebelled after more than thirty years of being coiled in a fight-or-flight mode. "Whatever I was able to endure emotionally stored itself in my muscles and began to poison me."

Karen finally sought professional help. The long, arduous process of therapy and self-help was almost as painful as the past she was fleeing. The denial she had been using as a survival weapon would have to be discarded, and the spectres of her childhood terrors faced in all their ugly reality. Together with her daughter, Karen has emerged victorious.

What is it in Karen that allowed her to survive her ordeal? What qualities did she possess that gave her the resources to pull herself out of the legacy of perversion and destruction? Why is she now a successful business woman, when one of her sisters turned to drugs and alcohol. Why did she not choose the path of her other sister into an austere life of poverty and religious fervor, or her brother's descent into drugs and alcoholism?

What qualities in Karen pushed her to aspire to more than mere survival? She changed her perspective!

EXERCISES ON PERSPECTIVE

1) Think of a recent setback. What is it?_____

_____

_____

2) What happened? _____

_____

_____

3) What resources do you need to overcome it?

_____

_____

_____

4) What have you learned from this? What alternative pathways could have been taken?_____

_____

_____

5) What do you need now so that it doesn't happen again?_____

_____

_____

6) What could you do differently in the next similar situation?_____

_____

_____

Chapter Nine

INITIATIVE

Even when confronted with a hopeless situation you still have a chance to make it meaningful. . . . in turning personal tragedy into a triumph or by transforming your predicament to an accomplishment.

Victor Frankl

A crisis occurs on a passenger liner in the middle of the Atlantic. The lives of hundreds of people are dependent upon the choices being made in the next few minutes. Dozens of crewmen report to their posts. Damage control assesses the situation and the crew springs into action. This can make the difference between a temporary crisis and a permanent tragedy.

What we as individuals do under similar circumstances is as crucial. The Champion has his own internal damage control. The Champion does not wait for the proverbial "someone to do something." He *is* that someone.

Thomas Peters and Robert Waterman (1982) credit "a bias for action," as one of the eight attributes of excellent companies in their book. "Getting on with it," is a hallmark of successful business, and "even though these companies may be analytical in their approach to decision making, they are not paralyzed by the fact."

Businesses are composed of people. It is the people who have the bias for action that make these companies so successful. What can determine success in an individual determines it in a business.

It is this "bias for action," which appears again and again in our Champions. I call it "initiative." Webster's New World Dictionary (1988) defines initiative as "the action of taking the first step or move; responsibility for beginning or originating." This definition describes the quality of initiative in

Champions beautifully; they have the knack of cutting through the cacophony of panic, fear, helplessness, and passivity to see what can be done. They have the initiative, according to Frankl, to turn a personal tragedy into a personal triumph or accomplishment.

"When my husband called and told me he had been laid off, my first reaction was to crumble," said Denise, a full-time mother with three children under six. "Inwardly I whined, 'What's going to happen to us?' I sat for two hours staring at the sink full of dirty dishes worrying about losing the house, the car, everything. Then I got to the point of thinking 'What are we going to do?' But I really didn't think about what we were going to do, I was thinking about what my husband should do. Finally I just said to myself, 'No, what am *I* going to do about this?' Well, for one, I told myself, you're going to do the dishes."

By the time Denise's husband came home, depressed and discouraged, Denise had made a list of all the things they were storing that they could sell for extra cash. She had cancelled the cable TV subscription, turned the heat down a notch, and had already begun marking the want-ads for baby sitting jobs. "Not only did I feel so much better by doing something, I was pretty proud of myself too. I know it meant a lot to my husband not to see me crying at the kitchen table when he came home."

The experience Denise gained by taking the initiative and seeing and feeling the paybacks has made her confident that she is up to whatever life hands her. "I can make dinner for five for under six dollars, and I now know how to change my own oil in the car," she says proudly. "I'm thinking of doing a magazine article with tips that I've learned so I can help some other woman who might be sitting crying at the kitchen table."

Those who cope most successfully with a painful experience are those who deal actively with the situation. They take responsibility for themselves. What works for one person may not work for another. Deciding what to do and how to do it is highly dependent upon the stress situation. The type of adversity is a major factor in the type of coping behavior. The initiative taken by a man struggling with divorce is very different from the initiative that might be taken by a woman coping with cancer.

If the situation is perceived as a challenge (fighting cancer), good copers use rational action (active participation in health care), perseverance, and self-adaptation, among others. Facing a loss, good copers tended to use a more cognitive method of action, such as prayer and faith, and the sharing of feelings.

As English essayist and novelist Aldous Huxley proclaimed, "Experience is not what happens to a man; it is what a man does with what happens to him." Huxley's own initiative or "bias for action" was instrumental in his success despite eye disease and blindness. Had the prolific writer waited for someone to do something about it, a myriad of beautiful thoughts and wise observations would never have been written.

For most of us, the law of inertia besets us on a daily basis. Just "getting moving" is the hard part — and that's when things are going smoothly!

According to Newton's Law of Inertia, objects in motion tend to stay in motion, and objects at rest tend to stay at rest. To stop motion takes an outside force, the greater the motion the greater the force. To move a body at rest takes an outside force, the greater the mass of the body, the greater the moving force must be.

Succumbing to inertia is very common and apparent in everyday life, but it occurs in more important contexts as well. When we succumb to inertia, we mentally rationalize why the task is not important. This differs from procrastination in that the procrastinator knows he will do it — eventually. "Each advance toward overcoming inertia can represent a developmental step of general significance, which may lead not only to increased freedom to develop new skills but also to increased satisfaction from these skills."

This predilection to work shows up in the lives of other Champions as a coping method for adversity. "I really think of work as a salvation in the sense that work anesthetizes one's problem," says Ved Mehta. Mehta, born in India, suffered a severe bout of meningitis at the age of four, which left him totally blind. "I feel most alive when I am working," he says. "It must have to do with all those years of idleness when I had nothing to do and I had this exaggerated sense of time passing by and my just falling behind in the world." Mehta took action to reverse the effects of his inertia, and threw himself into work. He was a staff writer for the *New York Times* for almost two decades and then, on a roll, went on to become a film maker.

Taking action makes the difference between a Champion and a spectator. We can dream all the dreams and have the noblest of motives, but without action, we do not progress upstream. Without the stroke of a paddle, we are swept downstream by the current despite our protests to the contrary. If change is to occur, then there must be action, and it can't wait for someone else.

David L. Evans, Senior Admissions Officer at Harvard, says, regarding the development of a frighteningly large black underclass, "We must stop talking and get moving."

Evans, who is black, understands that initiative is the quality of the Champion in action. He recommends action on the part of the individual to study and get an education, rather than engaging in analyses of structural problems within society. This, he says "could take us well into the next century. We simply cannot wait that long."

The Champion acts, takes control of his life. "We must convince black youngsters," says Evans, "that academic achievement, personal sacrifice and the other underpinnings of a productive lifestyle can lead to a strong self-esteem." Bingo!

Peter DeMorjian was a sixteen-year-old Cuban refugee living in America in the 1960s, fleeing from Fidel Castro. He had been jailed by the Communist government for conflicting ideology. Once in America Peter worked various hard labor jobs. Finally in 1968, he realized that the American dream was an illusion, and that he was going nowhere. He knew that without an education he would be doomed to spend the rest of his life at back-breaking itinerant labor and minimum wage, dead-end jobs. So he applied to the University of Notre Dame for admission and a student loan. He did so because he remembered reading about how they admitted and gave financial assistance to minorities. However, he was rejected by Notre Dame. But this did not stop Peter and he applied to Florida State for admission. Again, the rejection letter came. But this time he did not take no for an answer. "I saw the light with a burst," he says. "I knew I had to go there and plead my case." Peter hopped on a Greyhound bus and rode nine hours to the admissions office of the university. Peter wasn't about the let life just happen to him. Instead of accepting the university's refusal for admission, he did something. "I had to do something," he says. "Getting on that bus the next day was the only thing I could think of. I did it, and it worked." What if it hadn't worked? "I would have done something else," he relays matter-of-factly.

A wonderful by-product of initiative is the self-esteem it generates. As we discussed in the chapter on Confidence, self-esteem (positive self-image) is integrally tied into a feeling of control. By taking charge and doing something, confidence is buoyed and the likelihood of success is increased. In turn, a stronger sense of confidence increases the likelihood of action. Inaction not only ensures nothing will change or improve, it undermines our confidence. Can anyone afford to disregard almost a quarter of the qualities that we find in

Champions?

Initiative implies action, and Champions act on a problem or challenge, even if the problem appears to be something over which they have no control. They do not respond like Seligman's dogs who would not even try to find a way out of their predicament. They adapt their mental attitude and seek remedies and solutions. Then they do something about it. This simple call to action can eliminate much of the passive helplessness which is at best non-productive, and at worst, destructive.

Perhaps the feeling of well-being that we experience by being able to do something accounts for the incredible effort to support the war on the domestic front during WWII. Mothers, wives, and girlfriends donned hard hats and overalls and rallied to the defense machinery. Could this all be patriotism, or could it perhaps be an acting-out of their need to feel like they were doing something to protect their loved ones? They were focusing on remedies to the problem instead of their helplessness.

This active aspect of controlling the forces about us has a myriad of implications. If we teach our children the proper way to "fail," they will become much more likely to deal successfully with problems in the future. Several studies have found that children who focus on failure and what might have caused it were more likely to feel helpless. And feeling helpless, as Seligman's dogs have shown us, is a sure way to guarantee that the children will not even try any more. On the other hand, children who focus on remedies for the failure are much more likely to succeed in future tasks.

The most effective coping techniques used during periods of severe stress are those which are active in nature. Coping techniques which are inactive, such as avoidance coping, are associated with psychological distress. As the saying goes, you can't run away from your problems, because the running away is as deleterious as the problem. So you've got two problems!

Champions concede the futility of only one thing . . . running away from your problems. Instead, they turn and face them and (pay attention, this is the important part) *do something*. Merely facing them without appropriate action is like getting a good look at the tackle before he runs you over.

As I mentioned previously, initially feeling sorry for myself after my cancer surgery and pondering the prospects of living any sort of normal life with a colostomy, I quickly began turning my energy outward and began doing things. I investigated thoroughly the different types of post-operative treatment, and chose a new experimental therapy at the time, combining the surgery with radiation therapy, which is now a very prominent post-operative cancer treatment. I began writing several journal articles on how it felt to be an ostomate, and even joined an ostomy support group.

Another personal example of doing something in the face of adversity occurred after my divorce. I very quickly moved into a townhouse, trying to establish a new normal routine as quickly as possible, and began trying to re-establish the relationship that I had so tragically lost with my children. The point is that after each one of my setbacks, my divorce personally being more tragic than my cancer surgery, *I did something*, I focused on moving forward with my life.

"Putting together that scrapbook on Jerry's life couldn't make him come out of that coma," says Naomi, explaining how she coped with the loss of her son. "But I felt so helpless and I had to do something. I know it sounds silly, but I felt that by doing something — anything — I could keep from being swept away with him." Naomi intuitively understood the value of doing something, if only to maintain position until enough strength returns to allow forward progress. Her choice of remedies however was more than busy work; it was an appropriate way to remedy her fear of losing him forever. The scrapbook will help keep him in her memory more clearly.

In "Living Alone and Learning to Love It," Lou Glasse, president of the Older Women's League, sums up her prescription of coping with widowhood. "The rebound occurs when you take control of your life," she says, "and get active in improving your future."

Gertrude Curtis, a widow in her 80s is even more succinct. "You can enjoy it or be miserable," she states. She chooses to enjoy it by visiting nursing homes and hospital patients, attending daily church services, and playing nine holes of golf several times a week.

Gertrude's philosophy of just doing it is echoed by Frank Epperson, the man born with spina bifida previously mentioned in the chapter on Confidence. "It's not like my life is a poker hand and I can throw back two. This is the hand I was dealt," he says of life in a wheelchair. "I either play it or I fold. So I play it. What else is there to talk about?"

Indeed, too much analysis of the causes of our problems may divert our attention from doing something about them. In fact, this may explain the popularity of self-help and self-analysis. They can provide us with an excuse not to get down to the work at hand. By occupying our minds with theoretical busy-work, we rationalize our inaction — a sort of esoteric procrastination.

"When a stone trips us up, we do not fall to disputing its existence: we put it out of the way," stated essayist Leigh Hunt, over two centuries ago.

Hunt understood the realities of life, and the necessity to sometimes dismiss theoretical debate and causal analysis in favor of simply doing something. The same thoughts are echoed today by Rabbi Harold Kushner: "We need to get over the questions that focus on the past and the pain — 'Why did this happen to me?'—and ask instead the question which opens doors to the future: 'Now that this has happened, what shall I do about it?'"

Once we have decided what to do, the next step is doing it. And, as we have discussed, "doing it" often requires overcoming inertia. In any situation, getting things done requires discipline.

A story is told of one of music's true geniuses, pianist Ingace Paderewski. Following one of Paderewski's brilliant performances, an adulating fan gushed, "I'd give my life to play like that!" The virtuoso replied frankly, "I did."

What the fan lacked that Paderewski had was discipline — discipline to put his money where his mouth was. Paderewski had devoted his life to his music, not with words, but with deeds. Practice, practice and more practice, and the discipline to do it distinguish the Champions.

While the fan professed to want to play as brilliantly as Paderewski, his actions did not bear out his words. As Ralph Waldo Emerson put it, "Man's actions are the picture book of his creeds."

Our actions are evidence of our values. Just as an idea is not a book until it is written, a value comes into existence with action. I often hear from men and women who tell me that their families are the most important thing in their lives. And yet, the job, the yard, the football games, or the social obligations all get prime-time, to the exclusion of the family. "By your fruits you will know them," was Jesus' admonition almost two thousand years ago. Not much has changed.

If Paderewski had not disciplined himself to make the sacrifices necessary to act on what he deemed important, he would be no different from the fan in his audience who merely professed his ambition.

Discipline requires that we say no to the many temptations that lure us away from the doing of what we must. Even in the writing of this book, I had to exercise discipline in the face of temptation to relax in an easy chair with a good book that someone else had written. I had to resist the lure of tomorrow and reject the enticing Scarlett O'Hara School of Business: "I'll think about it tomorrow. Tomorrow is another day." But if I were to believe my own words back when I was fighting my cancer, that I wanted to write and to teach and to share my experiences, I knew I had to sit down and do it. If I didn't, then I would know my values were a sham.

To sit down and do it requires discipline. The very sound of the word strikes a harsh note, conjuring up images of humorless headmasters and cheerless great-aunts. It smacks of the tedious clicking of a metronome, the dull drone of memorized lines from "Beowulf," and the unnatural occupation of a young boy in a suit sitting motionless in church.

We need to get over the idea that discipline is punitive. In its pure sense, it is guiding and caring. Parents discipline their children to show them the right path, and they do it out of love. Self-discipline is affirming our love for ourselves.

Champions know that self-discipline is not self-flagellation. The purpose of self-discipline is to get what you want. In an interesting sense, self-discipline is really self-indulgence. By knuckling down and doing what you have to, you are fulfilling your fondest wishes. What better indulgence is there than to realize your dreams and aspirations?

If you are not yet convinced that getting down to business is the base avenue, consider this. Those who persist in well-planned orderly tasks report less stress-related illness. Here again is evidence of the physical benefits of having the qualities of a Champion, in addition to the emotional ones. Coming from "hardy stock" often translates as having ancestors who had a strong work ethic. They were industrious and probably quite healthy because of their diligence and discipline.

Discipline is not without sacrifice, but it's the trade off that makes it worthwhile. Champions know that what they sow today, they will reap tomorrow. The here and now is what determines the future.

If we take our cue from successful businesses, we see that action is the essential ingredient. Nearly three-quarters of the high-achievers researched by George and Alec Gallup for their book *The Great American Success Story* (1986) rank themselves as "very efficient" in accomplishing their tasks. Can one imagine a successful business that didn't accomplish anything?

Initiative requires us to sieze the moment. Amy Bjork Harris and Thomas Harris, M.D., point out in *Staying OK* (1985) that "much of our lives is spent preparing for distant tomorrows. While we are consumed with daily anxiety about tomorrow or next week we miss this moment, which will not come again."

Champions over adversity know how to sieze the moment. Painfully aware of the capricious winds of change, they do not count on favorable conditions tomorrow.

Initiative — the quality that allows us to harness our internal energies to do what has to be done. Are you a procrastinator? Too afraid of failure to even start? Overwhelmed by too many details? Following are some exercises to make molehills out of mountains, and the story of a Champion who did just that.

INITIATIVE

Something to Think About and Do

As a young boy, Peter DeMorjian was told by his father, "Look up to the north." The idealistic young Cuban, inspired by his father's words and the promise of the American dream, knew that one day he would study in the United States.

The DeMorjians lived a comfortable, middle-class existence in Cuba. Peter's father was a physician, and the DeMorjian children were able to attend private schools. The tightly knit family was content and secure, and the recurring unrest in the government was but a faint rumble which did not affect them much. There were lives to be led, patients to attend to, and food to be put on the table.

Then, on January 1, 1959, when Peter was sixteen years old, Fidel Castro and his guerilla army marched triumphantly into Havana. The Cuban Revolution had succeeded in overthrowing Fulgencio Batista.

At first the populace applauded the measures being taken by the new government. By May, the revolutionary and Marxist nature of Castro's regime was becoming apparent, and supporters of the liberator were increasingly disenchanted. It was becoming harder for the DeMorjians to ignore the impact of the new government on their lives. Through the Agrarian Reform Act, privately owned land was reapportioned to the government, and it became increasingly clear the direction this course was taking.

In late summer, Peter Morjian was attending Mass at his church where the parish priest was echoing the sentiments of much of the church. He railed against Fidel Castro's government and exhorted his parishioners to take a stand as well. Several armed men dressed in the unmistakable camouflage green of military fatigues interrupted the Mass, shouting down the priest with invectives and pro-Castro slogans.

"I exploded," says Peter. "I stood up and confronted them for disrupting the Mass. The whole thing escalated with people taking sides and shouting."

One of the priests took Peter's father aside and advised him to get Peter out of the church for his own safety. "I remember my father being angry," he says. "He felt that I had put myself and the family in danger."

Peter's father was right. The next day, the priest visited the DeMorjians and counseled them to find a way to get Peter out of Cuba. "They've been looking for him," the priest said grimly.

Desperate to send his son to safety, DeMorjian called upon an uncle who had been living in the United States since 1933. Calls were made on behalf of the boy and a student visa was obtained. Peter left Cuba on September 10, 1959.

Young and alone in a strange country, Peter was realizing his dream of studying in the United States. But savoring the dream was bittersweet, since he did not know when he would ever again return to his beloved home.

After one year of attending classes at Mars Hill University in North Carolina, the money his father had given him had run out. Unable to pay tuition or living expenses, Peter returned to Miami in search of work.

"It was very humbling," says Peter of his experiences. "Seven of us lived in a two-bedroom apartment. It was sometimes 100 degrees and very humid. With so little space, we took turns sleeping on the floor in the kitchen."

Peter took whatever work he could. "I scraped the rust off the hull of ships while they were in port. I picked tomatoes in the fields for $.60 an hour. I delivered newspapers, and worked as a bagboy in a supermarket. Anything. I needed the money to go back to school," he recalls.

The hard labor and the low pay were discouraging, but what weighed heaviest on Peter's mind was the prospect of never returning to his homeland, and Cuba had now broken off diplomatic relations. The United States forbade travel between the two countries.

So when Peter was approached by an organized band of Cuban refugees, led by former Cuban Prime Minister Miro Cardona, with a plan for reclaiming their country, Peter was listening. The plan was daring and exciting to the young man, and he joined with other exiles in enthusiastic support of this noble mission.

What could go wrong? The plan had the support of the United States. Training and arms were supplied by the CIA, and as Secretary of State Dean Rusk would testify, all U.S. agencies involved had unanimously recommended the attack.

"I was young and full of ideals," says Peter. "I wanted to free my country and have my home back."

The island of Cuba was scheduled for invasion on April 17, 1961. Fifteen hundred Cuban liberators would land at the Bay of Pigs.

Peter's role was in the pre-invasion infiltration team. He and his compatriots were smuggled into Cuba, where they dispersed to the hills and various strategic points. "Our job was to sabotage whatever we could," says Peter. "When the force landed we were to knock out oil depots, telephone lines, sabotage the railroads — everything."

The ill-fated invasion is now history. Most of the counter-revolutionaries were captured or killed within three days. Peter managed to go undetected for a full seven days, hiding out in the hills and foraging for food.

Eventually, he, too, was captured and thrown into prison, with over one thousand others. Peter was convicted in a public military trial of "crimes against the nation." He was sentenced to ten years in prison. "A light sentence," says Peter, "because I was young and had no past ties with the former government." He saw many of his friends sentenced to twenty and thirty years each. Others were shot.

Peter would be nearly thirty years old when his sentence was up. The hopeful young man with the ambitious dreams could now only see dank prison walls and listen to the buzzing of the flies swarming about in the sweltering humidity. "The conditions were very bad," recalls Peter. "Some of us were in solitary confinement two, three, even five months at a time."

The middle-class young man now longed for what was once hardship in the United States. The thought of one of the juicy ripe tomatoes he had picked for $.60 an hour taunted him as he considered his meager rations. Scant portions of thin soup and a bit of rice were all he had to sustain him. His hunger allowed him to ignore the insects crawling about in the food.

The provisions for hygiene were virtually non-existent, and medical care was all but disregarded. Inadequate nutrition and filthy conditions took their toll. "There was much dysentery," says Peter, "and very many toothaches. There were a lot of medical problems."

Peter tried to maintain his health and his sanity. In his tiny cell, he exercised both his body and his mind. "I wrote letters on whatever I could and we would smuggle them out," Peter says. "I played games in my mind, doing mathematical equations, trying to recall facts from history. I relived childhood memories. And," he adds, "I did a lot of dreaming about the future."

Rumors spread throughout the prison about negotiations with the United States for the prisoners' release. By February of 1962 the prison grapevine filtered news about a trade of prisoners for supplies, despite the U.S. refusal in 1961 to Castro's demand for 500 tractors in exchange for the prisoners. In

March, the rumors intensified when several of the prisoners were sent to President Kennedy to convey the terms of the release offered by Castro.

In June, the prisoners received confirmation of the negotiations and were bolstered by the knowledge that the United States and Cuba were now at the bargaining table. The intolerable conditions were made more tolerable for Peter with the glimmer of hope for an end in sight. Peter could stand it another day and another day.

By September, it became apparent that something was up. Conditions began to improve. It was still an oppressively hot, filthy prison, but Peter could tell that efforts were being made to improve their conditions. Two months later, unaware of the Cuban missile crisis, his suspicions were confirmed. Guards told him he "would be home for Christmas."

December 21, Peter and the remaining prisoners were exchanged for 53 million dollars worth of medical supplies and baby food. A jubilant Peter returned to the United States.

For awhile, freedom was sufficient. His entire family was now in the United States, having fled during the crisis. Peter's youngest sister was in Portland, Oregon, with a foster family under a program sponsored by the church in the United States to aid refugees. Peter's father, now sixty-three-years-old and unable to work as a physician in the United States, worked to support his family picking tomatoes in the fields as Peter had done.

Peter, too, worked hard at any odd job he could get. Miami was filled with Cuban refugees, and wages reflected the abundance of cheap labor.

In 1968, Peter realized that the American dream was an illusion, and that he was going nowhere. He knew that without the education his father had wanted for him, he was doomed to spend his life at back-breaking itinerant labor and minimum wage, dead-end jobs.

Peter recalled a program he had seen about the University of Notre Dame. In it was the story of a young man whose father, like Peter's father, dreamed of an education for his son. Like the DeMorjians, the family had no financial means to support this dream. "The man traded his cows and donkeys for money for tuition," recalls Peter. "And his son was able to go to Notre Dame. This boy went on the become the head of the university."

Inspired, Peter sat down and composed a letter to the Dean of Notre Dame. "I have no cows or donkeys to trade," he wrote, "but I will work harder than anyone you have ever seen."

He opened the letter he received in response to his plea with hopeful anticipation. The rejection was a form letter, and Peter's hope crumbled. Discouraged and disillusioned, Peter continued work at the warehouse.

It wasn't long before he looked around him and again decided that a higher education was the only way to pull himself out of his rut. "Am I going to do this all my life?" he asked himself. "I said no I'm not going to do this! The environment will catch up with me."

He applied to Florida State University for a student loan. Again, the rejection letter came. But this time he did not take no for an answer. "I saw the light with a burst," he says. "I knew I had to go there and plead my case." Peter hopped a greyhound bus and rode nine hours to Tampa, where he asked to see the Admissions officer.

"I'm coming here to ask for admission," he said clutching the University's letter of rejection. The admissions officer listened and then told Peter they would reconsider. Heartened, Peter returned to his warehouse job in Miami and resumed work while awaiting the decision. The personnel director of Jordan Marsh where he worked sent a letter of recommendation to the University, testifying to the boy's hard-working nature.

After an anxious wait, Peter received the word. He had been accepted. "I guess they liked my approach," he says. Peter lost no time in getting started on his studies.

Peter was true to his word, and the university did like his approach. Despite carrying a more-than-full curriculum, and working nights and weekends, Peter managed to get his degree in three years.

Upon graduation, Peter took a job with Gulf Oil, with whom he stayed for four years. He went on to secure increasingly better positions with a bank, a construction company, and then Citicorp, one of the world's largest banks, where he works today.

The world of finance is a long way from the prisons of Castro's Cuba and the fields where he and his father picked tomatoes. But Peter DeMorjian does not look back. The journey upstream has taken too long and too much from Peter for him to look down the river.

What qualities did Peter have that gave him the strength to survive the demoralizing and physically brutal rigors of Castro's prison? What did Peter have within him that kept him going through the discouraging years of minimum wage, hard labor, and disappointment? What made Peter take to the river and paddle relentlessly upstream, always looking up "up to the North?"

AN EIGHT STEP PRESCRIPTION
FOR PROCRASTINATORS

1) Choose one thing that you have been putting off. Make sure that it's specific and not vague. Select something concrete and real that you'd like to do.

   _____

   _____

2) Ask yourself why you should stop procrastinating. Make a list of the advantages of putting this task off.

   _____   _____

   _____   _____

   _____   _____

3) Make a list of the disadvantages of putting this task off.

   _____   _____

   _____   _____

   _____   _____

4) Now, weigh the advantages of procrastinating against the disadvantages. Ask yourself whether the costs or the benefits of putting it off are greater.

   _____

   _____

   _____

5) Now make a similar list of the advantages and disadvantages of getting started on the task today.

           Advantage   Disadvantage

   _____   _____

   _____   _____

   _____   _____

6) Think about the task that you have now decided to do. Now list any problems or obstacles that could sabotage your good intentions, and the solutions to these problems beside them.

            Problem   Solution

_____   _____

_____   _____

_____   _____

7) Break the job or task down into its smallest component parts, and concentrate on one part at a time. You can do this in one of the two following ways:

    I. Tackle the job or task in a step by step fashion.
        OR
    II. Work in short spurts (the Swiss Cheese Approach).

8) Lastly, think positively and give yourself credit for each small step once you've begun a job that you have been avoiding.

Chapter Ten

OPTIMISM

The pessimist sees the difficulty in every opportunity; the optimist, the opportunity in every difficulty.

L. P. Jack

One might consider optimism in the face of tragedy an impossibility. How can it be suggested that the mother of a dying infant "look on the bright side"?

Eighteenth century English journalist and poet James Henry Leigh Hunt, who had many of his own adversities to suffer, speaks eloquently of the incomparable sorrow that comes with the loss of a child:

"A Grecian Philosopher, being asked why he wept for the death of his son, since the sorrow was in vain, replied, 'I weep on that very account,' and his answer became his wisdom. It is only for sophists to pretend that we, whose eyes contain the fountain of tears, need never give way to them ... Sorrow unlocks them in her balmy moods. The first burst may be bitter and overwhelming; but the soil on which they pour would be worse without them" (*Deaths of Little Children*).

Hunt goes on to provide some insight into how anyone can bear what many believe to be the harshest cruelty any parent could feel. "Those who have lost an infant are never, as it were, without an infant child. They are the only persons who retain it always ... The other children grow up to manhood and womanhood, and suffer all the changes of mortality. This one alone is rendered an immortal child. Death has arrested it with its kindly harshness, and blessed it into an eternal image of youth and innocence."

The wonderful thought of having our child with us always is a touching answer to the question of what good could possibly come from the death of a child. What opportunity might this tragedy provide? The chance to really know our own hearts, and to understand the fleeting nature of life; or we may learn how to truly appreciate a young life, to form patience and tenderness with another child.

What mother would spare herself her grief by trading away her time of joy with him? The child's life brought love, and death will not deny that love. Is that not something good?

Optimism is not a blind disregard for reality. It is merely one of the views we may take of reality, the perspective of choice for those who would rather be happy than unhappy. As Sir Winston Churchill said, "I am an optimist. It does not seem too much use being anything else." Is it cold outside or is it brisk? Is the cup half-full or half-empty? Are you very old or have you lived very long? Is the house cozy or small?

Champions over adversity share the quality of optimism. They see tragedy in a way that others do not. They see possibilities, and they see the prospect of something good coming from bad. They see, as L. P. Jack said above, "the opportunity in every difficulty." At the very least, optimists see the bad not continuing. As Annie said in the Broadway musical *Annie*, "The sun will come up tomorrow."

Dr. Denis Waitley defines optimism in the context of positive self-expectancy. "Self-expectancy," he says, "is a self-fulfilling prophecy. It is the idea that what you fear or expect most will likely come to pass."

Optimism, then, is expecting the best. Pessimism is expecting the worst. And researchers believe that optimism and pessimism are formed in relation to *why* we think good or bad happens. How we explain the misfortune or failure that occurs can be the key.

"Explanatory style" is a term psychologists use to describe the way people explain bad things that happen to them. By looking at explanatory styles, we can readily see how they shape our attitudes of optimism and pessimism, and how they, in effect will determine what we do from there.

Martin E.P. Seligman is the father of the explanatory style theory. For twenty years, he has worked and developed his theory to where it has become a remarkably accurate predictor of success or failure. The explanatory style theory grew out of Seligman's learned helplessness theory, which we discussed in the chapter on Confidence, and is now referred to by psychologists as the revised helplessness theory.

Optimists, says Seligman, have an explanatory style which characterizes their adversity as external (it's not necessarily my fault), specific (it was a direct result of this factor), and unstable (this is temporary). Pessimists, on the other hand, have an opposite explanatory style. They see things as internal (it's all my fault), global (this always happens), and stable (it will always happen like this).

To illustrate, imagine two divorced men. One says, "No wonder Edith left. I'm a jerk. I'll always be a jerk." Another says, "Emily left me for her own reasons. She needed something from the marriage that she did not see in me. Perhaps I'll meet someone who will see what she needs in me."

The optimist is obvious. He's the one who explains things as having an external cause which is specific and temporary, and he's much more likely to bounce back.

The pessimist however, gets down on himself and sees the situation as very likely to repeat itself. He's also more apt to be depressed. Over 100 experiments with over 15,000 subjects have explored and confirmed that a pessimistic explanatory style is related to depression. Subjects who gave mainly stable (This always happens), global (I can't do anything right) and internal (It was all my fault) explanations for a bad event were consistently more depressed than those who offered the optimistic explanatory style.

An external explanatory style (It's not my fault) can also be viewed in relation to the "just world" theory, which suggests that we need to believe that people get what they deserve and deserve what they get.

This works as an external explanatory in that the cause is something outside of us, i.e., justice. It also serves as a pretty good optimistic explanatory style providing you are not the victim. The optimism is derived from the belief that you haven't done anything to deserve adversity, so you're pretty much safe.

A related theory of "defensive attribution" suggests that people assign causes for a misfortune to someone or something which will best enhance their feeling better about themselves. By ascribing a cause to adversity that allows you to let yourself off the hook — such as chance — you can maintain your self-esteem. Chance seems to be a fairly common cause for adversity attributed by good copers, including King Solomon who said in Proverbs, "Time and Chance befall us all."

Now I'm not telling you all this so you can identify the difference between an optimist and a pessimist. You can already distinguish the two quite handily without gumming up the works with labels like "explanatory style." I bring this up so that you can use the component parts of an optimist to help you develop a more positive attitude.

Everyone tells us, "Look on the bright side!" and yet no one tells us *how*. If we are accustomed to looking at things in a pessimistic way, we literally don't know how to look any other way. It's like telling someone to be more mature. Fine. Great advice. But *how*?

By knowing that optimists talk to themselves differently from the way pessimists talk to themselves, we can try learning their language. By dissecting the language of an optimist (analyzing his explanatory style) we can mimic its parts. That is how infants first learn to talk. They mimic sounds. And though the sounds don't make sense at first, eventually the child learns their meaning, and words become tools. By mimicking the language of the optimist, even if it doesn't make sense at first, we can learn to be optimists, too.

Here are some suggestions to help one develop an optimistic point of view.

1) Imagine a recent setback or failing. Sit down and write a paragraph about it, *honestly*, explaining why you think things went wrong.

2) Look at what you've written. Did you say that the cause was something within you as a person, or was it something outside of you? If you said it was something inside of you (I was stupid, or I had it coming to me, or I couldn't do it right) try rewording it with an external explanatory style. (There was more to this than the information I had; the situation was ripe; despite my best efforts, this situation demanded skills I have not yet acquired).

3) Did you say that the situation was something global? (They're all against me; the whole company is run by jerks; the world is full of evil.) If so, try rewording it with a more specific tag. (Bob started the false rumor that I was cheating on my expense account. This situation was not handled well. Though most people are basically good, this man acted maliciously).

4) Did you say that the situation was something stable (permanent)? (This always happens to me. The rich get richer and the poor get poorer. I'll never change.) Try rewording it to reflect a temporary view of the situation. (Next time will be different. Money earned and lost can be earned again and saved. There are aspects of my personality that I need to develop.)

5) Rid your vocabulary of absolute words that imply permanence.

WRONG	PREFERRED
poor (permanent)	broke, strapped, struggling (temporary)
stupid (permanent)	uninformed, unaware, unprepared (temporary)
weak (permanent)	still growing, still developing
hopeless (permanent)	bleak, grim, serious (still implies hope)

A word of caution regarding explanatory style: In noticing the tendency of optimists to attribute something outside of themselves as the cause of a difficulty, it might be tempting to conclude that if we wish to be optimistic, we should never blame ourselves. To an extent, that may work. If nothing is ever your fault, it is certainly much easier to look on the bright side. (Hey, don't blame me for getting cancer from smoking cigarettes. It's the cigarette company's fault for letting me buy them.)

Watch out, however, for blaming everything on someone else. Aside from not being very nice — you'll lose the friends you'll need for Chapter Ten — it's also not very healthy. There is a positive correlation between finger-pointers and maladjustment. Malcontents blame their condition on financial situations, family life, lack of opportunity, and a lousy social life. They are not a happy bunch even though they aren't down on themselves.

Self-blame is often the healthier route. Blame directed at one's own behavior correlates with a lack of depressive symptoms. I think the middle ground is most often taken by Champions who take responsibility for the behavior but do not attribute blame to an innate character trait.

By adapting a completely external style of explaining adversity, we take away our feeling of control. (If it's always someone else's fault, then I can't do anything about it.) We need to be able to take control of our lives, and if it's all in someone else's hands, we can't. If we blame "family life" or "finances" for a problem, we brush over the real picture. Just who makes up this family — aren't you included? And just whose finances are these, anyway? A completely external explanatory style requires a denial of the many other qualities of a Champion. I do not suggest that optimism is a romp through life without blame or fault.

To properly use the language of the optimist for our own purpose — to develop the qualities of a Champion — let's extract the reasonable portion and leave the rest. The reasonable portion of using an external explanatory style is this: Do not blame yourself *as a person*. It is certainly right and constructive to acknowledge your part in a problem, and entirely appropriate in many cases to say something like, "What I did was stupid." See how this differs from putting your very self as the cause? "I am stupid" attacks you as a person. "What I did was stupid" affixes the blame where it belongs — on an action or a response, which is a temporary situation.

A word of caution regarding optimism: Optimism, if it is to be useful to us, must be seasoned with a pinch of reality. It may be comforting to clap wildly along with Peter Pan proclaiming, "I *do* believe in fairies! I do, I do, I do!" but it is hardly as therapeutic for us as it was for Tinkerbell.

Merely looking for the best and wishing for the best does not make it so. Indeed, a positive attitude will increase the possibilities of good, but will not necessarily create them. For every optimistic thought we should have a plan. The man who sits blissfully awaiting his ship to come in had better have launched one.

Not surprisingly, irrational beliefs can exacerbate an already stressful situation. Paddling upstream is hard enough without worrying about the next river, or if your canoe will spring a leak, or if an electrical storm will hit. Both physical and emotional distress are much more likely to surface when change occurs in one's life while accompanied by thoughts of dire consequences that might come out of the change.

"I am an old man and have known a great many troubles, but most of them have never happened," said Mark Twain about the whole unproductive business of worry and pessimism. Life's continual surprise-party of roadblocks, hills and mountains should keep us busy enough without having to invent problems. Besides, it's just plain unhealthy. Those with a pessimistic view of unfortunate experiences around age twenty-five tend to have poorer physical health at age forty-five. Similarly, stamina in later years has been directly traced to a healthy, positive outlook during periods of adversity.

A new branch of medical science called psychoneuroimmunology explores the relationship of mental attitude with the body's own resistance to disease. As we have seen in previous chapters, many doctors and researchers believe that a positive mental attitude directly affects the body's natural ability to heal itself.

Stress can weaken the human immune system. In a study which involved drawing blood from students several times during the school year, and again at exam time, the researchers found a correlation between stress and the body's defenses. Interferon, a naturally produced protein that inhibits the growth of viral infections was significantly lower during stress.

In a study of thirty-two people whose homes were damaged or destroyed by fire, those who coped best had found something positive in what had happened, and also were less likely to place blame for the tragedy.

What could you possibly find positive in coming home to a pile of ashes? Many people find that their sense of gratitude that no one was killed is a very positive emotion. An increased feeling of family unity, an anticipation of rebuilding, and a new perspective on the value of *lives* versus *things* can all be positive, optimistic viewpoints. By not blaming anyone ("You left the iron on and now my house is gone!" or "I told you we should have gotten a lightning rod!") the Champions do not compound the damage by wounding themselves and others around them.

Do you look for the difficulty in every opportunity, or the opportunity in every difficulty? Can you see sunbeams streaming through dark clouds after the rain? A positive mental attitude opens doors of success for those who will but reach out for the opportunity to grow. Read about Gloria Estafan's return to the stage and practice the exercises on Optimism.

OPTIMISM

Something to Think About and Do

On March 20th, 1990, Gloria Estefan was at the height of her career. Her band, the Miami Sound Machine, had sold over 10 million albums worldwide over the previous five years; their current LP, "Cuts Both Ways", was sitting comfortably on the charts, and the band was finishing the first leg of their world tour. They were in their tour bus on the way to a concert in Syracuse after making a short stop in Washington, D.C., to play at a benefit concert in support of the government's fight against drug abuse.

"That day everything was perfect. I was in the best shape, physically. My husband, Emilio, and son, Nayib, were with me. The tour was sold out everywhere. I was looking forward to the gig in Syracuse. And I love the bus. I always used to say, if you crash at least you're not falling 37,000 feet."

Six people were aboard when Gloria curled up for a nap on a couch in the forward cabin. Around noon she awoke when the bus stopped behind a stalled tractor-trailer on Interstate 80, near Tobyhanna, Pennsylvania, twenty miles southeast of Scranton. Moments later her tour bus was struck from behind by a speeding semi, slamming the bus into the truck ahead.

"The next thing I knew I was on the floor. The impact knocked Emilio right out of his shoes. I tried to lift my legs, but they would only go so far. I told Emilio I broke my back, but he tried to reassure me, 'No, baby, maybe you just pulled a muscle.' I can remember thinking that I would rather die than be paralyzed.

"I told myself, 'No way am I accepting this.' Then I realized, 'As long as I can move my feet even a little bit, I must not be paralyzed.' "

While waiting nearly an hour for help to arrive, Gloria clung on to Nayib, nine, who broke his collarbone in the crash.

"He was very brave. I think that he was really worried for me. Knowing he was not badly hurt helped me. If something had happened to him, I couldn't have handled it."

Paramedics had to lift Gloria through a smashed front windshield because the bus door was inches from a steep embankment. Next came an anxious forty-five-minute ambulance ride through ice and snow to a Scranton hospital. She was in horrifying pain that was relieved very little by morphine injections.

"The pain was so excruciating. I picked a spot on the ceiling and focused on it, like they teach in childbirth classes. But believe me, I would rather have given birth to ten kids in a row than go through that kind of pain again."

Once stabilized, she was quickly flown to the New York Hospital for Joint Diseases and Orthopedic Institute. There she underwent delicate spinal surgery. The operation lasted four hours and required a bone graft from Gloria's hip and the insertion of steel rods to shore up the fractured vertebrae. Although the rods are permanent, they were located in a section of the spine that flexes very little anyway, and would not inhibit Gloria's movements. The operation left a fourteen-inch scar down the middle of her back.

"The plastic surgeon who closed me up said he was getting religious after my accident. He said that my spine was so mauled that I shouldn't have been able to move."

But overcoming adversity was not new to Gloria. This dynamic Cuban-born singer is one of the Miami exile community's triumphant American dream stories. She was not quite two years old when her father — who was a motorcycle escort to the wife of former Cuban President Fulgencio Batista — and her mother, a schoolteacher, arrived penniless in Miami. When her father became bedridden and ill, due to Agent Orange poisoning in Vietnam, Gloria, then age eleven, took care of him. In addition to taking care of him, her other responsibilities included caring for her younger sister and helping her mother learn English. Gloria was a high school honor student, who earned a partial scholarship to the University of Miami, where she graduated with degrees in psychology and communications in 1978.

A month after her accident Gloria was already working out three days a week, rebuilding her strength and flexibility with the help of her exercise machines and personal trainer. She credits her optimistic and determined attitude to "return to the stage better than ever" to the love of her husband and the more than 4,000 floral arrangements, 3,000 telegrams, and 30,000 postcards and letters she received from friends and fans.

"It definitely helped. So many people concentrating positively and praying for me. It was like an energy I could feel. It helped me bear all the pain."

Gloria's workouts were very painful to her, yet she continued to fight to make it back to the recording studio and stage. "Performing is one of the best feelings I know."

However, her personal trainer, Carmen Klepper, noted that recovery can be especially difficult for a patient whose body has always been a very sound machine and in good shape. He stated, "Imagine someone who is in great shape who suddenly cannot walk. Mentally, that can crush you. Your body crumbles. But Gloria is recuperating faster than anyone. She has a drive like I have never seen."

Gloria suffered through an unbearable amount of pain for several months on the trek that was destined to place her back in the rock-and-roll limelight. Gloria made her triumphant return to the stage during the 1991 American Music Awards show, which was nationally televised live in late January, 1991. She sang a song from the new album that she and the Miami Sound Machine recently recorded. Gloria is back, no doubt, better than ever.

EXERCISES YOU CAN USE TO DEVELOP
AN OPTIMISTIC VIEWPOINT

1) Force yourself to find at least one good thing in a relationship, problem, or confrontation. Have you learned a valuable lesson?_____
   If you answered yes, what is it?_____
   _____
   _____

   Did this compel you to look at yourself more honestly?_____
   _____
   _____

   Did you develop a stronger sense of compassion as a result of this situation?
   _____

   Or humility?_____

   Did you gain a greater appreciation for someone?_____
   _____

2) Make a written list of all the good things that could come as a result of a current problem. For example, if the problem is a serious financial crunch, your list could look like this:
   A) I am learning the difference between needs and wants. Actually, I need very little. The wants are what got me into trouble.
   B) I am learning greater responsibility.
   C) I am ridding my life of non-essentials.
   D) Since I can no longer afford to pay for entertainment, our family is becoming closer.
   E) I am more compassionate of the poor, realizing that finances do not determine human value.
   F) I am becoming creative and resourceful in finding ways to make do, etc.

Now you make your list:

A. _____

_____

B. _____

_____

C. _____

_____

D. _____

_____

E. _____

_____

F. _____

_____

3) Compliment someone today. Praise a task well done. Acknowledge a kindness! Look for the good. Then find a reason to compliment yourself.

4) Read or listen to something upbeat. For a day, try not listening to the news or reading the newspaper — it's 95% negative. Turn off the soap opera!

5) Make a list of all your accomplishments, however small. Add to it each day. List five now:

A. _____
B. _____
C. _____
D. _____
E. _____

6) Seek out other optimists. Avoid negative people. They'll drag you down. Complainers, gripers, doom-sayers, and worriers need an ear. Don't give them yours.

7) Sing or hum. If the dog howls, put him outside. (See #6)

NETWORK OF SUPPORT

Life is a chronicle of Friendship. Friends create the world anew each day. Without their loving care, courage would not suffice to keep hearts strong for life.

Helen Keller

As a culture, civilized man is a social being. We *need* other people, pure and simple.

Everything ever written has in some way to do with a relationship: man's relationship to his fellow man, his family, his community, his God, his environment. Even when something is ostensibly written about man's relationship with himself, it invariably exists in relation to others.

When deprived of human contact, people literally wither and die. The widower, left alone after forty years of marriage, who becomes ill and dies within months of his wife's death, is a frequently factual parable. The child deprived of human contact and parental affection becomes withdrawn and developmentally delayed. We never outgrow the need for relationships, and our development can be arrested at any time during our lifetime when those relationships disappear.

Studies also indicate that close relationships have a positive affect on life expectancy. In fact, the mortality rate is 2.5 times higher for those who did not have social bonds. Other studies have produced similar results. Studies also show that unmarried people, who have few friends or relatives, and who are not involved in community activities, have more than twice the mortality rate of those with social contacts.

Human contact is the mirror that reflects our self-image back to us. Without it, we can never truly know ourselves. What nicer self-image can we have than one of a person who is loved? Knowing there are people pulling for you can provide enormous strength. An outpouring of love and support gives a person someone else to lean on, and the comfort of knowing he is not alone.

Knowing that there are so many who care is a wonderful tonic for diminishing confidence, a frequent consequence of adversity. As we discussed earlier, an ailing self-image is a Champion's worst enemy. A network of support buoys that self-image by reinforcing our worth.

Champions understand the importance of relationships, both for a healthy outlook on life and for indispensable allies in time of adversity. A network of support is the safety net that can keep us from hitting the pavement when we fall, or the trampoline which bounces us up time and time again. A network of support gives us the courage to keep our hearts strong for life, as Helen Keller stated at the beginning of this chapter.

Research shows that mothers with more children had better post-divorce adjustment, along with the children. The researchers attribute the successful coping to the social skills and inter-activities among the family members.

A strong family bond is perhaps the richest natural resource that the Champion draws upon. Time and time again we hear of the foundations laid by parents for a successful life. As I have mentioned previously, the family bond between my parents, me, and my sister grew significantly stronger during the time of my illness. This is a bond that has remained strong ever since.

Growing up with a family that taught him to consider his blindness as a bother, not a tragedy, David Hartman always believed that he could do what he set out to do. His father would respond to his continual questions about his limits with, "You'll never know unless you try."

From baseball to wrestling to vice president of Student Council in high school, and then off to Gettysburg College, where he graduated Summa Cum Laude, David tried and succeeded.

His next goal was to become a doctor. Although he seemed to be the only one at times who really believed in his ability to become a physician, David was blind only to the doubts of others. Accepted by Temple University after nine rejections, David plunged headlong into the exhausting studies that cause sighted but less strong willed students to fail. In 1976 he received his M.D. degree.

Were it not for the unfailing support of his family during his childhood, the support of hundreds of volunteers from Recordings for the Blind, Inc., and the help of other students' eyes to get him through such classes as "Neuroscopic Tissue Structures," David's will and determination would not have been so decisive. He credits his parents, Fred and Idamae, and his sister Bobbie, with his can-do attitude, as well as the support and encouragement of his wife, Cheri.

For press Secretary James Brady, the outpouring of support from an entire nation after the assassination attempt sent a clear message of hope to the stricken man. He received over 70,000 pieces of mail in the eight months he spent in the hospital. Friends began a tradition of catered Friday night dinners in his hospital room, and a city turned out to welcome him home upon his release. But the strongest support came from his wife, Sarah. "Without Sarah," says Brady's nurse, Susan Deyo, "Jim would never have done as well as he did."

A strong support system of family can insulate us from the negative expectations of society, and the attendant cruelty that comes with it. Sadly, there are those who believe that life's happiness exists in finite, exhaustible supply. Someone else's adversity or unhappiness serves to assure them that this short supply is not being wasted on others. They rationalize that other people's problems increase the likelihood of their own good fortune.

Families and loved ones, however, tend not to take this jaded view, and take their measure of joy and satisfaction from the joy and achievements of those close to them.

Born weighing only three pounds, Geri Jewell was pronounced dead at birth. At eighteen months, she was diagnosed as having cerebral palsy, a result of brain damage to the central nervous system.

Despite the resulting difficulties controlling speech and physical body movements, Geri decided on a career in which only a very few succeed — acting. She started as a stand-up comic, a brutal undertaking for the thin-skinned. Geri's lifelong exposure to stares and ridicule prepared her for the tough audiences in comedy clubs, and her unusual situation gained her plenty of attention. Soon, she landed a part on TV's "Facts of Life."

Geri is convinced that if she had relied on society's expectations for her, she would never have begun to tap her potential. "I resent people for letting me get away with all of it," she says in an interview with Edwin Miller (1982), "because I had to pay a price in the end. If it weren't for the way I was treated at home, I would be a total emotional cripple today."

Her parents insisted she do chores like the rest of the children, and leg braces were discouraged in favor of exercise and hard work. "Two words that weren't permitted to come out of my mouth as long as I was at home," she says, "were 'I can't.' "

Like Geri's parents, this "hands-off" approach is typical of the families of Champions. They understand the importance of individual self-image, and encourage it by encouraging their children to be responsible for their own happiness.

Dick Van Arsdale credits his parents with a major role in his development. Unlike many "sports parents," Dick's parents were the cheerleaders, not the coaches. "My parents did not force me to participate in sports," Dick says. "They provided equipment and a great deal of support. They rarely missed any of our games. I knew they cared very much."

Arthur Ashe experienced the same kind of parental support. Although his mother died when he was six, Ashe grew in the warmth of encouragement from his father. "My father was positively instrumental," he asserts. "He was not a 'Little League' parent."

Vincent Dooley, present athletic director and former head football coach of the Georgia Bulldogs echoes the "hands-off" approach to parental support. "My parents played no major role in my sports development except to teach me some important basic values that apply to sports and life in general."

This assurance of unconditional love and acceptance is very important to anyone taking risks and reaching out for a goal. It is crucial when coping with adversity.

Perhaps a focus on the adversity, rather than the solution, tends to occur when there is a support system of people who either enjoy talking about the misfortune, or who dwell on it in the belief that they are comforting you.

This might explain the unexpected results of a fascinating study at Tennessee State University. The study set out to reconfirm the notion that those with social support and/or personal resources were less vulnerable to depression. What emerged, however, were findings that indicated that those who used the most support were the most depressed, and the most adversely affected by stressful events (Husaini & Van Frank, 1985).

Gerri Jewell believes that her family and friends' support was totally responsible for her success. And yet, there are millions of people whose family and friends care equally — without the same results. The differences between those people and Champions may be the willingness to accept that support.

Each day another parent or spouse finds a suicide note or a drug overdose.

Anguished hearts bleed pain for the loved one who turned from the love and support that was there for them. Unable to accept love or ask for a shoulder, the suffering becomes unbearable and oblivion is preferable to life.

Champions accept the gift of compassion and understanding. Like all gifts, the giver intends it to be used and not put on a shelf or sent back unopened.

For some of us, the love, support and encouragement of family and friends is not enough. This is not due to any shortcoming on their part. In some instances, the support can only come from someone who has been there, who truly understands your situation because he has experienced it himself.

The phenomenal success of Alcoholics Anonymous is due to the powerful interaction between those who know, from the depths of their souls, just what you are going through. While well-meaning friends and loving family can exhort the alcoholic to just "get a grip on himself" and "kick the habit," only the recovered alcoholic can tell him how. Only the recovered or recovering alcoholic can empathize with the anguish of withdrawal and the daily struggle to stay sober.

For alcoholics, it is important for them to know that they are not alone, that there are millions of others in the same situation who have gone through — and triumphed over — what they are experiencing.

Support groups as an organized effort for self-help are a relatively new phenomenon, but the premise is not. Down through the ages, people have knit together, joined by a common adversity. In Biblical times, the Jews comprised their own huge support group of those who worshipped the God of Abraham in the face of slavery, exile, and persecution. Early Christians gathered together in secret to bolster each others' faith against brutal persecution.

The proliferation of organized support groups today is due in part to the immense network of communication available to us. We can *find* other people with much greater ease. Secondly, the decline of the nuclear and extended family, along with the mobility of society, has left a need that was once filled by family, friends, and community. Neighborhoods are now largely composed of transient strangers, and we eschew the once prevalent code of getting involved. Indeed, one need only open the phone book for a listing of groups that can put you in touch with others who can empathize.

Following my cancer surgery I reluctantly joined the Ostomy Association. I quickly developed a new appreciation for such support groups and the several hundred others like it. I will always treasure the love, friendship, and support shown to me by my fellow ostomy members from the first meeting I attended to the present. I feel certain that from this group I have made several friends for life. Not just friends, but brothers and sisters. I have the confidence and knowledge that if I ever have any problems or concerns dealing with my colostomy, my dear friends from the Ostomy Association will always be there to help me.

Candlelighters Childhood Cancer Foundation was formed by Grace Powers Monaco out of her need to be an active participant in the care of her baby daughter, Kathleen, who had leukemia. With Dr. Sanford Leikin, chief of pediatric hematology-oncology at Children's Hospital in Washington, D.C., she formed the beginnings of a worldwide organization which offers hope, encouragement, and solid facts to frightened and bewildered parents.

"If you're thinking of others, you're less likely to submit to the temptation of pity and self despair," says David Guttman, Ph.D., author of *Reclaimed Powers*.

S.O.S. (Survivors of Suicide) is a support group for the family and friends left behind by people who have taken their own lives. Diane Tolliver describes how the group helped her come to grips with her uncle's death. "No one can really understand what it is like to be left without a clue. The 'whys?' are just overwhelming. Only someone who has had a person close to them commit suicide can begin to understand."

After three meetings with S.O.S., Diane knew that she had gotten what she needed from the compassion, understanding, and suggestions for coping from the group. Others will remain in the group for years before they can make it on their own. Some will remain indefinitely, helping the newcomers' fresh wounds to heal, and in doing so, know they are once again productive and needed. Their pain and adversity was turned into an opportunity to help their fellow man.

Like any medicine, however, there is a danger in continuing dosage after the need has passed. As Denis Waitley points out in his book *The Winner's Edge* (1980), "Traditional psychotherapy has in many ways been a great disservice to the improvement of the healthy outlook of people undergoing treatment. By replaying the past and dredging up memories and by looking back at the probable causes of deviant behavior, little more has been done other than focusing on that behavior, rationalizing it, and perhaps even fixing the blame for it."

Support groups can effect the same sort of wheel-spinning if there is a reliance on them as a place to go to rehash and lick wounds over and over. Their value lies in strengthening the participant to go on with life.

All of the Champions I've seen recognize the difference between engaging in group self-pity, and using the support group to pull oneself out of it.

Frank Epperson, the paraplegic wheelchair racer mentioned previously, is involved in a Handicap Awareness Panel which speaks primarily to school-age youths about the disabled. For him, the value of this support group is the opportunity to educate others. The group's focus is on change rather than plight.

Theresa Saldana, the actress who survived a knife attack at the hands of a deranged fan, understands both the strengths and the weaknesses of support groups. "For six years I was involved in the victims' rights movement almost exclusively," she says. "That was, and still is, a great experience. But it got to the point where . . . I was over-exposed and over-involved. It was great to take a horrible experience and do something positive and creative with it, but," she says, "I am not a professional victim."

Only you can determine if your support group is contributing to your growth or if it is hindering it. The group can be effective only insofar as its members desire healing and forward progress. Just as I suggested in the chapter on Optimism, rid your life of negative influences. If the support group you attend fits that description, it's time to leave. A good support group is like a good parent: it prepares the child to go off on his own.

German theologian Franz Rosenzweig, who became paralyzed at the age of thirty-six wrote, "None of us has solid ground under his feet; each of us is only held up by the neighborly hands grasping him by the scruff, with the result that we are each held up by the next man, and often, indeed most of the time, we hold each other up."

Barn raisings, quilting bees, and canning parties were ways our colonial ancestors coped with the difficulties of frontier life and held each other up. They understood that they needed each other to survive. Read about a woman whose friends and family helped her create a new life. Practice the exercises following to make your own network of relationships richer.

NETWORK OF SUPPORT

Something to Think About and Do

Mitzi Brown sits in her living room in a fashionable area of St. Paul, relaxed and comfortable amid the bustle of activity. Her granddaughter coos contentedly in the infant seat on the couch while the TV announcer blares the play-by-play of the football game. One of Mitzi's daughters, babysitting for her niece, chats on the phone. The boarder pops his head around the corner and says he'd like to pay the rent now. Mitzi is obviously in her element; she is content and happy surrounded by family and activity.

She can look back with satisfaction on her life — raising four happy children in an equally happy marriage, with a house full of laughter and activity where the door was always open to friends. It's the American dream of the fifties, where Mom is always home, dinner's in the oven, and Dad's shirts are all neatly ironed.

To the casual observer, Mitzi Brown is like a million other women. Sixty-one years old. Housewife. Mother. Grandmother. With sixty-one years of happy memories of family and friends.

Only Mitzi Brown isn't like a million other women, and she has only thirty-four years of memories — patchwork painstakingly crafted from scratch and embroided with mere shreds from her past.

Mitzi was twenty-seven years old, vibrant, pretty, and full of life. She had married her high-school sweetheart and was the mother of two adorable children, ages four and seven. She and her husband Pat had been looking forward to the night out to celebrate their friend, Rich's, birthday.

The relentless rain for the past three days couldn't dampen their spirits. The birthday dance had been such fun, and the party was to continue at their friend's house. Laughing and joking, the three couples piled into Rich's car. Spirits were high, and they looked forward to enjoying the birthday cake Mitzi had bought earlier that day.

The road was slick, and the car was traveling at a high rate of speed as it went into the turn. Unable to hold the curve, the tires slid into the muddy shoulder, slipping and skidding out of control. The car flipped over and slammed violently into a telephone pole. The guide wire sliced through the convertible like a cheese cutter. And then there was only the sound of the driving rain.

The flashing red lights of the police cars and ambulances pierced the blackness of the night. Pat Brown was wandering in the darkness, calling for his wife. Rich lay in the mud, his head beneath the overturned car. Rescue workers teamed to lift the car, and as they did, one of the officers leaned his body against the car and put his hand into the mud to brace himself. His hand met the body of Mitzi Brown.

"If that officer had not felt me in the mud," says Mitzi, "they would have pulled Rich out and then dropped the car back down on me. I was lucky."

Ambulances rushed the young couples to the hospital. Mitzi was the most seriously injured, and she was not expected to live. Her scalp had been sliced from her head by what police officers presume was the metal framework of the convertible top. She lay in a deep coma, a coma from which doctors said she would never emerge.

Her parish priest stayed with her family, offering what little hope and solace he could, hope which the doctors would not offer. They had sewn her scalp back on with just a few coarse stitches; a cursory effort, since she was not expected to live through the night. Neatness wouldn't count. They stabilized her vital signs as best they could. Mitzi labored for breath through the tracheostomy, a hole in her throat that doctors had surgically incised to provide an airway. Mitzi's smashed and broken hand was left untreated. To reconstruct the mangled parts would have been a pointless exercise, for doctors knew Mitzi would never awake to use her hand again.

Medical science had served Mitzi Brown as best it could in 1954. Now, all they could do was wait. Miraculously, Mitzi did not die that first night. Nor the second night. With each succeeding night, Pat and her family grew more hopeful. They watched and waited as the dark-haired beauty lay clinging to life through tubes.

Doctors tried to prepare Mitzi's family for the inevitable. If she did live, she would undoubtedly be a "vegetable." The brain damage was too extensive to hope for Mitzi to regain any of her faculties. She would, they predicted, simply "curl up into the fetal position," and live out her days in her own silent prison.

More than a month after the accident, Mitzi astounded the hospital staff. She opened her eyes. But there was no recognition in them. She was unaware of her surroundings, and she did not speak. She simply lay there as doctors had predicted.

Family and friends, along with the hospital staff, did everything they could think of to spark some sign of awareness in her. They dangled earrings in front of her, trying to get her to focus her eyes and follow the movement. They chatted endlessly in hopes of striking a chord in Mitzi. Slowly, very slowly, she began to show signs of "coming around."

Mitzi relates an incident her mother told her had occurred during those first weeks of gradual awakening. "The room was filled with flowers, and an arrangement of roses was brought in. I held out my hand as if I wanted one, so my mother placed one in my hand. She turned to sit down in the chair, and when she turned back, she saw me eating the rose." Mitzi laughs at the visual image. "I thought it was food! Of course, that upset everyone to no end. But that shows you how primitive I was at the time. I didn't know that a rose wasn't food."

Most upsetting to Pat was Mitzi's total lack of recognition of her husband and of her two sons. There was no memory of her children, nor of the marriage to her high school sweetheart. As Mitzi gradually became more aware of activity around her, and began speaking in simple, halting phrases, it became painfully apparent that Mitzi Brown had lost her memory.

To Mitzi, Pat was no more than just "a very nice man who seemed to be around a lot."

"I remember Mitzi looking at me intently one day from the hospital bed," Pat recalls. "She said that she thought it would nice if we got married some day. I leaned over and said 'Mitzi . . . I'm your husband!' "

"Of course, I didn't even know what husband meant at that time," Mitzi explains. "I'm not even sure why those words even came to me. There must have been some vague understanding of the concept for me to have said it."

In a desperate attempt to jar Mitzi's memory of her children, Pat defied hospital rules, and tried to bring the children to their mother. Pat knew this was something he had to do for the children as much as for Mitzi. The children had been told by schoolmates and neighbors that their mother had died. Three months after the accident, the children still had not seen their mother, and it was becoming increasingly difficult to console them. Pat had to prove to them that she was still alive.

Pat drove the family car into the back parking lot of St. Luke's Hospital and brought the boys to the window of Mitzi's basement-floor room. He raised the window to let them climb in. The cold November air rushed into the room, alerting an indignant nurse to the ruse. She scolded Pat for "trying to give Mitzi pneumonia," and shooed them all out.

Later, in an apparent change of heart, the nurse arranged a rendezvous in the hospital cafeteria. She told Pat to bring the children down and to buy them dinner. She would arrange for Mitzi to be brought down to the cafeteria, and to have her dinner tray delivered to her. The Brown family sat at the cold Formica table and ate their first meal together in three months. But Mitzi did not know her own children. All she knew was that she was having a "nice time" with this "very nice man" and the two little boys named Dennis and Jeff.

Once she was strong enough to leave the hospital for a few hours, doctors suggested that Pat take her on a little drive through familiar areas, and stop at their home. It was hoped that the familiar surroundings might trigger a memory.

When she walked into her house on Lake Johanna, her younger sister Kay was there tending to her newborn baby. "Ohhhh . . . that's why I am in the hospital," Mitzi said quietly. "I have a baby."

The flash of recognition, the instant flip of the switch that would turn on the light in Mitzi's mind did not come. Her family's hopes for the return of Mitzi Brown to their lives were further dimmed.

Mitzi was little more than a child. Totally dependent upon the people around her, she did not even know enough to ask to use the bathroom. Anything she did was in response to a directive. "I did what I was told. I didn't know enough to think for myself, so I simply did what people told me to do," Mitzi says. "It did not occur to me to do anything except sit there or lie there."

One day in the hospital, a nurse came in to check on Mitzi. The normally placid patient was surly and disagreeable, the first sign of any mood other than passiveness. "Get out of here and don't bother me," Mitzi ordered the nurse. "I'm talking to Mother Mary. Leave me alone."

Alarmed, the nurse left to summon the doctor. They returned to find that Mitzi's scowl had been replaced by a peaceful smile. "Mother Mary came to see me," she told them. "She was so beautiful! And she told me that I was going to get well and that I would be going home soon."

The staff of the Catholic Hospital was divided on what this all meant. Was Mitzi hallucinating, or had the Virgin Mary really come to visit?

Eight hundred miles away in Cincinnati, Mitzi's father believed. Each morning before work, he had been stopping at the church across the street from his office. There he knelt in prayer before the stone statue of the Virgin Mary. One of the statue's hands, like his daughter's, was smashed and broken.

Today, in looking back on the incident, Mitzi herself does not know what to make of it. She does not recall what happened in that hospital room. Mitzi points out that her own mother's name is Mary, but that neither she nor anyone else had ever called her "Mother Mary."

Eventually, Mitzi recovered enough to go home. Medically, all that could be done for her had been done. There were no programs or therapies in which Mitzi could be treated to help her regain her memory. She was simply sent home, a child leaving the hospital to begin a life with her new family.

For months after arriving home, Mitzi's life consisted of sitting in a chair in the living room. She would waken, and someone in the family would help her get dressed. Then she would pass the hours in her chair until six o'clock, at which time she went off to bed.

"I kind of wondered why I went to bed and no one else did," Mitzi says. "But it really didn't occur to me to question it. I wasn't doing anything anyway, so it didn't bother me."

While her sister Kay, who had moved in with her family to take care of Mitzi and the children, tended to the business of the house, Mitzi would sit and stare at the television screen. Though her gaze was fixed in the direction of the set, she did not comprehend. Mitzi did not read, either, because her eyes would not focus properly, and because she lacked the attention span. In addition, she could not understand much of the printed word. Reading comprehension is predicated on a certain level of cultural literacy, most of which had been erased by the brain damage. While Mitzi still had the capability to recognize individual letters and words, her mind could not interpret the message. Even the simplest of references would escape Mitzi's understanding. A story about two rabbits journeying to New York City on an airplane might as well have been written in Greek. She had no frame of reference defining what a rabbit was, what New York City was, or what an airplane was.

Despite that, every now and then, Mitzi would use words or phrases that indicated this knowledge was still there somewhere, locked inside of her. Traces would slip through the prison bars of her mind.

"I barely, just barely, remember sitting in that chair one day and looking at Kay," Mitzi recalls, struggling with the memory. "I sighed deeply and said, 'You are so good to me. I appreciate how kind you've been. But now I think I'd like to see my sister. I think I have a sister somewhere.' Kay got this very puzzled, quizzical look on her face and she said, 'Honey, I'm your sister. I'm your sister Kay.'" With that, Mitzi leaned back in her chair and sighed contentedly. "Oh, that's good," she said.

For months, Mitzi remained in her chair, a familiar-looking stranger living in the same house with her family. While Kay tried to bring a sense of normalcy to the household — cooking, cleaning, and tending to the passive woman in the chair — Mitzi's world was a simple existence. Even the pain in her broken hand that had been left untreated was not enough to stimulate an interest in what had happened to her.

"I knew my hand hurt, but I didn't know why," Mitzi says. "It didn't occur to me to care why. Nothing occurred to me at all as being out of the ordinary. It didn't even occur to me to wonder about the children. I saw them, and I knew they were there, and everyone told me they were my children. But I didn't know enough to feel a sense of loss about not understanding that they were mine."

Although she had been told she had been in a car accident, the meaning didn't register. One day she looked into the mirror, studying the reflection of the dark hair growing back in sparse little patches on her head. "Why did I cut my hair so short?" she commented absently. "I don't like it at all."

The first glimmer of the awakening came on a Sunday near Christmas time. Her entire family was gathered at the house, including her mother and father. Conversation and activity bustled about Mitzi as she sat quietly in her chair. Suddenly she bolted from her chair, and rushed to the front door. She leaned over and jerked the rag rug from the threshold and began shaking it vigorously out the door. "This is the dirtiest rug I've ever seen!" she exclaimed indignantly.

"My mother cried," Mitzi says. "That was the first time I had shown any interest whatsoever in doing anything at all. Everyone was thrilled."

Gradually, Mitzi began to show more interest in learning how to do things. Like a child, she began asking questions and trying to do things for herself. She was not allowed to do much around the house, for fear she would hurt herself. But like a little girl eager to help, she watched and observed. Pat would bring home groceries and lay them out. "This is a pork chop," he would say. "And this is an egg."

"There wasn't one specific moment when the light came on and I was normal again," Mitzi explains. "It was just a very slow, gradual process. Nothing just clicked. It just sneaked up on me and things slowly began to make sense. Whether or not it was my memory coming back, I don't know, because I was learning these things all over again. But as far as I was concerned, I was learning them for the first time."

Family and friends showered her with information, and Mitzi was increasingly eager for anything to fill the void in her mind. She continually asked questions and sought to understand all the things about her life that other people knew. She could only accept that the things they told her were correct, and trusted that what she was learning about herself was true.

With the help of her family and friends, Mitzi began to construct a facsimile of her past. Stories and recollections told to her were pieced together to form a framework on which to build her life. The names of friends were constantly paraded before her, along with a history of the relationship. Anecdotes from school, photos of the children, and a continuous barrage on who, what, and where threatened to put Mitzi on overload. But she desperately wanted to know.

"Once I intellectually understood that I had lived a life prior to the accident, I desperately missed it. I missed being able to remember. I felt terrible. I still feel terrible that there are so many things gone from my life."

It is difficult if not impossible for Mitzi to know to what extent her memory returned. Since the process of returning to "normal" was painfully gradual, she cannot sort out which of her "memories" are her own recollections dredged from the damaged recesses of her mind, and which have been assimilated by repetition, stories told over and over by family and friends. Mitzi ponders the dilemma. "You don't know what you've forgotten until someone says you have forgotten such-and-such. You never know for sure what you don't know because you can't know something if you've forgotten it." She laughs at the circuitous logic. And yet one senses the still nagging feeling of frustration with the quandary.

Pat explains how he looks at it. "It's like when you're a little kid. You think you remember something you said or did when you were three or four, because someone told you about it. You keep hearing the story over and over. Then you start thinking you actually remember, but in reality you don't. You have only taken other people's recollections and made them your own."

Mitzi continued to build a past with the bits and pieces of information she gathered from others. Marilyn, the wife of the friend whose birthday they had been celebrating the night of the accident, was Mitzi's constant source of data. "I must have called her thirty times a day saying, 'Now, who is so-and-so, and who is she married to?' Or I'd call her and ask her, 'Marilyn, have I ever been to California?' And she would patiently answer all my questions and explain to me who someone was, or describe what I had seen in California."

Mitzi spent hours poring through scrapbooks and baby books. The pre-school drawings and the Mother's Day cards pressed between the pages were pressed into her heart. With the boys on her lap, she hugged them hard, squeezing what memories she could from them, aching to feel what a mother should feel.

With each succeeding day, Mitzi would learn a new skill, however simple, and learn a new fact about her life. She wanted to do more. Finally, the day came when she would be allowed to work in the kitchen. Pat patiently went through the steps one by one, laying out the bacon in the frying pan, and showing her how to crack the eggs.

Mitzi tells about the first time she ironed. "All the neighbor ladies gathered in the house, set up the ironing board, and went through the process for me. Then they all sat around and watched me iron. That was the day's activity. They were all so excited for me. It was a very big deal. I was so proud of myself, and I was so pleased to be doing something that made everyone so happy. That's how simple my world was at that time," she says.

Mitzi continued to make progress, all the while asking questions. "I would call up Marilyn and ask her how to make coffee. Once I realized I could do things if I set my mind to it, I just wanted to keep doing more. Everything was new and exciting to me."

Eventually, Mitzi was able to begin caring for herself and her family on her own. As she steadily improved, gaining new skills each day, there awakened in her a nagging sense of dissatisfaction. While she couldn't put her finger on it at the time, she now knows that she had grown increasingly uncomfortable with feeling "different."

Everything seemed to exist in relationship to the accident. Everyone's conversation seemed to revolve around the accident as a sort of landmark in time. Family and friends would speak about things happening "B.A." or "A.A." — before and after the accident. The accident became the nucleus of not only Mitzi's life, but of everyone around her.

Pat and Mitzi discussed it, and decided that in order to escape this cycle, they should move to a new neighborhood. Two years after the accident, the Browns moved to their present neighborhood, a place where no one knew about Mitzi's ordeal.

"I do remember feeling somewhat embarrassed about getting out and doing things with people who didn't know what had happened to me," Mitzi says. "I was afraid they might think I was strange or that something was wrong with me."

Shortly after their move, Mitzi returned to the doctor who had first seen her after the accident. "He just couldn't believe it. He couldn't believe that I had just walked into his office, much less sat there and carried on a conversation with him."

It has been thirty-four years since Mitzi Brown lay in a coma. Today, she has four grown children and a deep feeling of satisfaction in the performance of her role as wife, mother, and grandmother. Mitzi was able to steer her derailed life back onto the tracks she was following before the accident. The values of family and faith gradually reawakened in her, and Mitzi Brown will hear nothing of being "just a housewife." For Mitzi, being just a housewife is the most important accomplishment of her life.

What made Mitzi struggle through the shadows of a past she could not remember in search of the past she would not surrender? What qualities did she possess that drove her to pull herself from the peaceful complacency of her chair into a frightening world of unfamiliarity? Without even knowing what a paddle was, how did Mitzi Brown pick hers up and travel in the upstream journey home?

EXERCISES TO DEVELOP A NETWORK OF SUPPORT

1) Cultivate and nurture your friendships. Be there for them if they are there for you. Write them a note. Send them a card. Clip a news item that would interest them. Visit them. Invite them to your house. Talk with them.

2) Spend time with your family. We find time for those things most important to us, so give of your time to show how important they are to you. Put down the newspaper. Cancel the meeting.

3) Tell loved ones how much they mean to you. Don't assume they know.

4) Learn the fine art of apology and forgiveness.

5) Extend the same patience and courtesy to your family and friends as you do to your co-workers. We tolerate more indignities from strangers than we do those close to us. How odd!

6) Listen — really listen to what your family and friends say. Ask questions about what they think.

7) Show an interest in other people's lives — joys and sorrows.

8) Extend kindness and thoughtful gifts of self. Clean house for an ill friend. Be a chauffeur or an errand boy if it will help. Send a gift from your garden, kitchen, workshop, or creative hand.

9) Keep in touch with friends far away; even friends you have not spoken with for years will be thrilled to hear from you.

10) Business contacts, peers, colleagues are all potential resources. Stay on good terms with them, even your competitors.

11) If you commit yourself to anything — a deadline, confidentiality, a committee — follow through. Reliability can pay dividends.

12) Do not burn your bridges. You may have to cross that river again.

Chapter Twelve

SPIRITUALITY

What a strange power religion is, how difficult for us to estimate its strength.

Llewelyn Powys

The influence of faith on a person's life is readily apparent. We all know people, or have heard stories about people, whose belief was so unshakable that it empowered them to overcome crippling tragedy or adversity. One cannot help but wonder if this "strange power," as Powys refers to it, is as real as those mechanisms we quantify in carefully controlled studies.

Religion has been a part of the story of man since recorded time. Indeed, the religions of the world provide our most ancient record of human thought. The universality of man's spiritual longings are evidence enough of our spiritual nature, and testimony to what may be the essence of humanity.

"The study of religion reveals that an important feature of it is a longing for value in life, a belief that life is not accidental and meaningless," says writer Geoffrey Parrinder in his book *World Religions From Ancient History to the Present* (1983). "The search for meaning leads to faith in a power greater than the human, and finally to a universal or superhuman mind which has the intention and will to maintain the highest values of human life."

Spirituality is perhaps the most encompassing of all the qualities of a Champion. It embodies the power of the universe in faith, hope, and love for a Supreme being — and can provide *all* of the qualities of a Champion.

Our spirituality, manifested by a faith in something greater than ourselves, provides *confidence* by putting us in touch with our divine nature. What greater self-image can we have than knowing we are created in the image and likeness of God? Our sense of control is strengthened with the faith that we have God's strength and power at our disposal.

For many, personal adversity challenges the very foundations of religious faith. Faced with an inexplicable tragedy — the death of a child, loss of a limb, inoperable cancer — the loving God in whom we've trusted and to whom we've prayed can be a sadistic figure to our grieving minds. "God's will" becomes a sentence to be served instead of a comforting strength. Or, faced with the paradox of a loving God overseeing a world of pain, the once-faithful might come to the conclusion that there is no God.

If confidence is evidenced by a lack of stress, what better stress-buster is there than the peace and serenity that come from faith? Observe those with true faith and you will find confidence.

In our discussion of the quality of *heart*, we saw that courage was a mark of a Champion. Nothing imbues the spirit with courage more than God's spiritual faith. The history books are full of stories about men and women whose courage enabled them to do extraordinary things, and the source of their courage was a strong faith in God. Joan of Arc, David, Moses, Abraham, the apostles, Mother Theresa, the Early Christian martyrs, the Jews of Nazi Germany—all of them were imbued with courage born of faith. And each day, even as you read this, miracles of courage are being performed by people who have a strong belief in their God.

Faith opens our hearts with trust, so we may learn and grow. This is the very soul of *adaptability*. Faith gives us the reality that there is so much more out there to know, and sets no limits. For those with a strong belief, adaptability is a natural by-product of the willingness to turn their lives over to God, to be shaped by His hand. "Change" is a word of hope, not something to be feared.

The basic quality in a Champion, from which the others leap, are *motivation*, goals, mission, purpose, and vision. For one in touch with his spiritual self, his motivation is clear. He need not spend his life wandering about, searching for that magic destination which will set his life on course. Faith provides the spiritual Champion every motivation, every reason for being that there is — life itself. The values that spring from goals are clear, and often are prescribed by religious affiliation. The person with faith has a singular purpose — to love and be loved by God.

Perspective is another quality of a Champion that a person of faith has. Perspective is seeing things in their true proportions and in relation to everything else. To have a view from eternity amid the infinite boundaries of the universe, we cannot help but see things in a different light. Faith brings us humility born of the realization that we are not the center of the universe. Those with faith have learned how to look at things through new eyes.

And what about *initiative*? As we have seen, Champions exhibit qualities of initiative. They are self-starters and take responsibility for acting on their beliefs and doing what is necessary. Faith can be the spark which ignites that initiative. Burning with the energy of their faith, believers are compelled to act upon them. Indeed, it is basic to many religions to measure faith by deeds. As we discussed in the chapter on initiative, our action or inaction is determined by our values. What better foundation for action is a value system based on faith in God? Initiative born of faith has the advantage of being inexhaustible. Even when results are not readily evident, those with faith continue to act, undiscouraged by the lack of immediate paybacks. Their faith assures them that their actions will be fruitful.

Remember, in the chapter on *optimism*, our discussion of explanatory style? We found that optimists tended to explain, or attribute, their setbacks to causes that were external, specific and unstable (temporary).

Faith in God provides all the necessary ingredients for an optimistic explanatory style. "God's will" provides the believer with an external cause for his adversity. He is able to attribute the adversity to a specific cause (test of faith, a mysterious purpose God has for him, a lesson). Faith allows the individual to see his adversity as temporary, since the very essence of faith is the belief in a merciful God who will deliver us from our travails.

The result of this faith is hope. Hope is spiritual optimism. No wonder those with a deep, abiding faith in God have the Champion's quality of optimism.

Finally, those with faith have a built-in *Network of Support* with an ever-present ally — God. This network of support is not reliant on visiting hours, group meeting schedules, or previous commitments. God is never too busy or preoccupied with his own problems. Those with faith have a kindly father, a comforting friend, and a healing physician at their side night and day. Beyond that, the spiritual Champion has likely built a network of support among his or her family and friends as a part of the process of living that faith. The family has long been a center of religious strength and solidarity. Because of this, people with a strong faith usually have existing family, community and social bonds. The network of support will usually mirror the same faith.

With all the qualities of a Champion flowing from the one quality of faith, it would seem expedient to concentrate on the spiritual aspect of self if we are to "train" ourselves to handle adversity. Unfortunately, that is the one quality of a Champion that defies quantification. We can talk about what faith can *do*, but we can't come up with an owner's manual with step-by-step instructions on how to "have" faith. I believe that the great spiritual writings of the prophets and disciples contain the wisest advice, and I do not presume to enter their domain.

All I can suggest is the notion that *we become what we think about the most*. We discussed this in the chapter on *confidence*. By focusing our thoughts and filling our minds with spiritual things, we become more spiritual. Whether faith can be "bred" in this manner, I cannot say. But the evidence of a spiritual quality in Champions is undeniable.

President and Mrs. George Bush found solace in their faith when they lost their daughter, Robin, to leukemia, two months short of her fourth birthday. "We were heartbroken, but we tried to find comfort in God, to accept and learn from our sorrow," George recalls in an interview.

"Each night, George and I pray aloud together before bedtime, and once a day we quietly read from either the Old Testament or New Testament," says Barbara Bush. "What is darkness without light? We have an obligation to balance the scales as much as possible."

Forgiveness

Some Champions' adversity has come in the form of something that was *done to* them, rather than something that has happened.

Forgiveness is a quality of spiritual insight that has enormous healing qualities. Theology professor, Lewis B. Smedes, in his book, *Forgive And Forget: Healing the Hurts We Don't Deserve*, points out that the destructive power of a wrong continues to do damage long after the wrong has been done. The hurting continues in the painful stream of memories.

Champions have the capacity for forgiveness. Pope John Paul II met his would-be assassin, Mehmet Ali Agca, face to face in Rebibbia prison to do what he knew he must. He forgave the man who tried to kill him, expecting no less of himself than the Shepherd whose flock he serves as its temporal leader.

Elizabeth and Frank Morris discovered the healing power of forgiveness. Writer Peter Michelmore describes their story in *Could They Forgive Their Son's Killer*? They were consumed with only a desire for revenge against the drunk driver who killed their only son, Ted. For nearly two years, their anger, grief, and pain at the loss of their son was funneled into the driver's trial and the efforts of Mothers Against Drunk Driving (MADD). Elizabeth's spiritual beliefs eventually drew her to the young man who killed her son. She visited him in jail, prayed with him, and told him she forgave him. Frank Morris forgave him a month later. "We forgave our son's killer because it was right," Michelmore quotes Frank as saying, "but we do not forget."

Through this forgiveness, the Morrises were able to come to terms with their own destructive elements — hatred — which had only made the loss of their son more painful.

Smedes acknowledges the unnaturalness of the act. "Our sense of fairness tells us that people should pay for the wrong they do." At the same time, he acknowledges the healing powers of forgiveness. Perhaps it is the unnaturalness of forgiving which gives it the power. By transcending instinct, we achieve a higher spiritual plane.

Karen, the incest victim who told her story earlier in the book, also shares this spiritual quality of forgiveness. While she has forgiven her father, her brother, and her mother for their roles in her hellish childhood, she still longs for the acknowledgment. "You never stop wanting them to say 'I'm sorry.' " Forgiveness is easier when forgiveness is asked. But Karen realized that forgiveness is an act of will, and therefore not dependent on anyone but herself.

Smedes offers his prescription for "the soul surgery we call forgiveness." He suggests:

1) "Confront your malice." Admitting our hate compels us to make a decision.

2) "Separate the wrongdoer from the wrong. Forgiving is finding a new vision of the person who has wronged us, the person—stripped of his sins—who really lives beneath the cloak of his wrongdoing."

3) "Let go of the past. Forgiving does not necessarily mean forgetting." Forgetting is a sign that the forgiveness has healed us.

4) "Don't give up on forgiveness. The hate habit is hard to break. As we do with other bad habits, we usually break it many times before we get rid of it altogether."

Many theologians and spiritual leaders believe that faith is a gift from God. If that is the case, then no amount of visualization exercises can conjure up the existence of faith. But I do believe that if faith is a gift, then we must at least open our hearts to prepare a place to receive it. One cannot take delivery on a package if he is not home to sign for it.

Are you ready to receive the gift of faith if you don't already have it? Is your heart open to forgiveness and that spark of God that is in each person? Read the story of spiritual help one man found in Alcoholics Anonymous's 12 Steps and practice the exercises to strengthen your own spiritual side.

SPIRITUALITY

Something To Think About And Do

On-camera at New York City's Channel 2 during the early winter of 1989, Jim Jensen, sixty-two, looked like a man on top of the world. An anchor at WCBS-TV for twenty-five years, this newsman was master of his trade, reporting the day's events with controlled authority. But away from his anchor desk his life was crumbling, his chemical addiction was about to catch up with him and force him into one of the toughest tests of his life.

It was not like he hadn't been through tough emotional tests before. In 1975 his marriage of twenty-six years ended in divorce and four years later his son Randy, a lawyer, was killed in a hang gliding accident.

Jim says, "My divorce and then my son's death were the beginning of what I call the spiraling down process. I didn't handle either one of them very well. I feel very strongly about marriage and believe in it very much, and when there was a divorce, I felt a lot of guilt. I never handle emotional things well at all. I was back to work a week after my son was killed. Everyone was telling me how brave I was. I didn't think that I was brave; I thought there was something wrong but I didn't know what. All I recall is that when I got the phone call from my daughter Lisa telling me that my son had been killed, my knees buckled. I got a tremendous pain in my stomach for a second. Then I wanted to throw the telephone through the wall. And then there was nothing."

After that Jim became more and more reclusive. He says that now he realizes that he was an addiction ready to happen, he was so empty then, looking for something to fill the void and kill the pain.

"I'll never forget that first time, at a party in the early '80s. It was very chic then. There was a lady at the party who said, 'Don't worry about cocaine. Nothing can happen to you.' What a mistake. Here I was such an intelligent person, doing something so hideously stupid. Next thing you know, I had a problem."

Jim was a solitary user. He used at home, especially on weekends. Along with his use of cocaine, Jim was also taking his daily dosage of valium that was prescribed to him four and a half years earlier for a sleep disorder caused by anxiety. He says that his valium addiction turned out to be more of a problem than his weekend use of cocaine. "I thought it was like aspirin tablets that I could take one whenever I felt like I needed one."

Jim says that he never went on the air stoned, but his conduct around the newsroom became erratic. His temper grew short, and he was very inconsistent in how he treated his fellow employees. He began missing work and family functions. He said that he used all of the excuses and lies, like a toothache that you had to go to the dentist for. "You think that you are fooling everybody, but you're fooling nobody."

It wasn't long after that his family and co-workers confronted him about his substance abuse and urged him to seek treatment.

"My eldest daughter, Denene, said during the intervention at the clinic where your family confronts you, 'Dad, I'm not here for you, I'm here for me. Because if you kill yourself, I don't want to feel guilty because maybe there was something that I didn't do. I don't want to feel guilty the rest of my life.'

"The heart of any addiction is denial, but when it's found out, and you are finally sent to a rehabilitation center, it's a great sense of relief.

"The treatment center was very Alcoholics Anonymous oriented. Alcohol was never a problem for me, but people with all kinds of addictions go to AA. At first I was very frightened to go, so some of the larger guys would actually surround me as we went in, so nobody would see me. It was so ludicrous. I was a scoffer, but these programs work. No longer are you a one-man gang. You have a mutual problem, and you are fighting to get over it. You also turn your life over to your concept of God. It's not a religious concept. It's spiritual."

After six weeks at the hospital, Jim's treatment was going well, and he was not having any signs of withdrawal, so he was discharged. He went to daily AA meetings and was feeling pretty good. He went back to his anchor chair at WCBS about a week later. Things were going well for Jim's first couple of days back at work, but he suddenly started having terrible pains in his legs and back. The cocaine withdrawal was over quick, but Jim's withdrawal from the valium had just begun, and it soon became a nightmare. He started getting only a couple hours of sleep a night, and began eating very little. He would be ice cold one minute and sweating the next. He says that he would go through three to four T-shirts a night that were soaked with sweat. "It was absolute, sheer hell."

"One of my daughters, Heidi, stayed with me in my place in Manhattan. She would get up with me at 3 A.M. and pour me a hot bath. She'd put hot towels on my legs and my back for the pain. She'd pray with me, encourage me, yell at me.

She was golden. But if you'd known her six or seven years ago, you'd never believe it. This wonderful, warm, sweet daughter was a fallen-down drunk, living on a bare floor in Houston. The family almost gave up on her. Finally, God intervened, and she came home and got into a recovery program. And she has been sober for almost seven years. Never did I dream that I would have to turn to my daughter. Daddies are supposed to be the source of help; kids are supposed to come to Daddy. But I had to go to my kids and ask for their help. That was a humbling experience.

"Last February was rock bottom. The valium withdrawal left me in a terrible depression, and shortly after my 25th anniversary party at the station, I had a monumental panic attack in the middle of the night. I went to walk on Madison Avenue at two o'clock in the morning in tremendous physical pain and absolute panic. I was hanging on parking meters to keep from falling down. I wanted to run, but I didn't know where. I was so depressed at that moment that I felt as though there was no future left, and that I might be better off dead."

The next morning Jim checked himself into a hospital in New York. He stayed there a month, and was then transferred to St. Mary's Hospital in Minneapolis. Since his release from St. Mary's he sees a psychiatrist once a week, and attends an AA meeting daily.

"I love to go to AA. It kept me alive, kept me sane, kept me on track. I made more friends in the last year than I had made in my whole life. People I can call up anytime of the night or day who will listen to me, and talk through a problem. It's a miracle from the Lord."

Jim returned to the TV station, not as an anchor, but as a reporter. He now takes more time off for himself. He has learned to appreciate the simpler things in life. He has learned to appreciate "living."

"Recently I celebrated Heidi's seventh anniversary of sobriety, and she celebrated my first. I'm now more than a whole year sober. I'm very proud of that. I'm so thankful to God and my family. For without them I couldn't have made it to where I am now, living life."

EXERCISES TO STRENGTHEN YOUR SPIRITUAL DIMENSION

1) Pray and meditate. Prayer is talking to God. For those who find it hard to comprehend that God can hear thought, consider how a man-made structure of metal, carbon, and silicone can pluck a living image from the atmosphere and place it in a box in your living room. Surely God can do at least as much as a TV.

2) Read the scriptures of your faith. To have a solid faith, you must know who and what you believe in. Only then will you know why.

3) Read the writings of the world's great philosophers and theologians. Your mind will be opened.

4) Talk openly with a loved one or a friend about your spiritual beliefs. Discussion often reveals things about yourself.

5) Talk to people whose faith you admire. They will be glad to share the source of their strength.

6) Religious services can reinforce a belief in the tenets of a particular religion, and can provide a comforting sense of continuity and tradition.

Chapter Thirteen

CLOSING THOUGHTS

Our chief want in life is somebody who will make us do what we can.

Ralph Waldo Emerson

The power of positive thinking has received a lot of exposure in the past decade. Countless books and articles have been written extolling the virtues of positive thinking. Untold millions have been made from the spreading of its gospel in seminars and on tapes.

Why is this such a popular notion? Probably because it appeals to the very basic need in us not to feel helpless. As we have discussed before, the feeling of helplessness is a very powerful agent in affecting our mental state.

It is very comforting to think that we can change our lives simply through sheer desire. No special talents are needed, no skills, no special tools. The amount of effort needed to produce a change is minimized in favor of the amount of desire.

It is no accident that the marketing focus for diet aids and get rich quick schemes appeal to the same instincts that motivate us to embrace the Power of Positive Thinking philosophy.

"Lose 20 to 50 pounds or more without dieting." "Eat all you want and stay slim." "Amazing miracle formula melts away fat while you sleep."

Billions of dollars have been spent on such claims, which are simply an appeal to the desire to belief that one can get something for nothing. Additionally, it comforts us by making us think that we are doing something to change our condition, and removes that sinking feeling of helplessness.

"Make $1000 a day working at your kitchen table." "Turn spare cash into big bucks." "Be a millionaire in six weeks."

Classified ads and solicitation mailers tout the financial power of their products, and clean up selling dreams to people who are grasping for hope. Unable to accept the gnawing feelings of helplessness, they feel better doing something—anything — and so they send for the secrets which will once again put them in control.

Without the necessary ancillary skills, positive thinking can become a disadvantage. It is not sufficient to practice believing that we can do something. We must expend some effort.

For those who do not act on good advice, the cycle can be harmful. With an ever-growing need for booster shots for their positive mental attitude, they eventually become increasingly discouraged because the realities of life do not measure up to their expectations. Convinced that it is their attitude that is at fault, they go back for another dose of Positive Mental Attitude (PMA). And so the cycle goes. High. Low. High. Low. Meanwhile, they have done nothing to change their behavior or their environment.

Consider the "No money down" real estate seminar explosion. The concept is a valid one, and no doubt made a lot of money for a number of people. Why, then, did these experts share their secret with millions of others? Because they know that learning a method is a very different thing from using a method. They know that most people, no matter how momentarily pumped up by the seminar, will not expend the effort needed to actually practice what's been preached.

Meanwhile, the students have a temporary feeling of well-being from having attended the seminar. They feel that they have taken control to make financial progress, and for a time will have escaped the debilitating effects of helplessness. Except for the very few who actually mobilize, this feeling of well-being is only temporary. Soon, in need of another attitude boost, they're off to the next panacea.

We become addicted to the medicine that is as bad as the disease. The very tools that purport to build a successful positive attitude often become the tools with which we dig into our own ruts.

We sometimes fool ourselves into believing that reading or hearing about the mistakes and victories of others is tantamount to learning the lessons contained in those stories. Nothing could be further from the truth. Exposing ourselves to knowledge does not ensure absorption of it, and it certainly does not ensure action.

How safe would you feel aboard a 747 piloted by people who had never flown a plane? Assume they have excellent credentials otherwise. They have read well over fifty books on flying, attended hundreds of hours of classroom lecture, and what's more, really believe they can do it. The person has a positive mental attitude. I know I would check out the Amtrak schedule.

So you see, it is not enough to have faith in yourself by virtue of a positive mental attitude. There must be other skills, skills borne of effort and determination.

None of the qualities discussed are by themselves sufficient to pull us up from adversity. They are intricately intertwined with one another. For some people, the quality of self-perception is stronger than the sense of direction, or the spiritual aspect of self may be stronger in one person than another. Yet there is a distinct interrelation among them. One cannot stand alone.

I am reminded of the story of the brave man who lived along the flood-swollen banks of the Ohio River. What seemed like forty days and forty nights of torrential rains had put the entire area in jeopardy. Local authorities came out to warn the river dweller to get to higher ground.

"Nope, I'm staying right here," said the man. "The Lord will provide."

The next day he was urged to leave his home immediately. The waters had entered the first floor.

"The Lord will provide," he maintained, steadfast in his faith.

The next morning, the water was rushing through his home. He clung to the rooftop as a motorboat came by.

"No!" the man protested. "I have faith in the Lord. He will provide."

An hour later, a helicopter flew overhead and lowered a rope ladder. "No!" he shouted over the din of the helicopter. "The Lord will provide."

As the helicopter flew away, the pilot tossed a life jacket to the man, which was promptly thrown into the raging waters.

Later, the man found himself at the Pearly Gates. Incredulous, he complained to the gatekeeper.

"All my life I've put my faith in the Lord," he protested. "I've not wavered for an instant. I believed God would provide for me in this hour of need and what happens? I drown!"

The gatekeeper shook his head. "He sent you three warnings; a lifeboat, a helicopter, and a life jacket. What MORE did you want?"

This man had a positive mental attitude and faith galore, but would not act on his beliefs.

I challenge you to action. If you believe what I have been saying throughout this book, and if you believe the people you have met in these pages, then act on what you have learned!

I challenge you to put your money where your mouth is. You say you want to grow in the qualities of a Champion. (You've said that by reading this book.) But our actions are what determine where our priorities lie. If you do not act on what you say you want, then you don't really want it. You've shown through your inaction that you are satisfied with the status quo.

If you don't take action, that's fine too. But be honest with yourself. Admit that you have chosen the path of least resistance. Don't play a game with yourself. Don't try to fool yourself into thinking that reading this book, or any other, is tantamount to growth or change. JUST DO IT!

Celebrate the distance travelled, not the destination. Following are some things for you to think about.

DISCUSSION AND REFLECTION

Some Things to Think About and Do

1) Adversity can be the catalyst which forces us into taking stock of our lives, either realizing we have no direction, or that our direction is faulty.

2) A goal need not be a thing, a station in life, or a tangible accomplishment. Sometimes the goal can be the journey itself in which we savor life's process.

3) Goals are not static. They must change and evolve as you grow, always reflecting your values.

4) Motivation is an inner drive, an impulse, or intention — all of these begin with "I." Your motives come from within — no one else can determine them.

5) Nothing of any value was ever achieved for the hell of it. There was a motive, a reason for the doing.

6) We look for excuses to avoid expending effort on things we don't feel strongly about.

Chapter Fourteen

WORKING TOWARD SUCCESS

MOTIVATIONAL PRODUCTS

THE CHAMPION WITHIN YOU
Audio Cassette Album

I have recorded an album of six (6) half-hour cassettes to complement this book, *The Champion Within You.* By listening to these recorded messages, you will be able to maintain a level of motivation that will give you the energy to overcome the obstacles in your life.

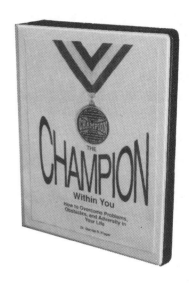

THE CHAMPION WITHIN YOU
BOOK AND MEDALLION

You may want to use additional copies of this book to give to others who are going through low periods in their lives. The printed word adds credence to thoughts and ideas. It may also be easier for you to express your support in this tangible way than by trying to talk about things that fall outside of the work relationship that you have with peers and associates.

STRESS STRATEGISTS
BOOK

In this book I have assembled chapters by numerous experts in the area of stress management. Some of them tell the author's personal story of surviving a stressful situation. In all chapters, the writer describes techniques that have been proven successful in turning stress into strength. It is the compilation of these different stories in different voices that makes the message so compelling.

"CHAMPION" LAPEL PIN

This handsome and high quality lapel pin will show everyone that you believe in yourself and that you are striving for the very best. You may also want to use it to reward your employees for the completion of some form of training or for the achievement of job performance goals. There are hundreds of other uses, some of which are mentioned in this chapter. Quantity discounts are available.

PERSISTENCE WALL PLAQUE

This famous quotation is a powerful message for salespeople and entrepreneurs of all kinds. It is printed in gold and black on high quality paper, measuring 18" x 24". It is available in a beautiful solid oak frame, or unframed.

"CHAMPION" RIBBON AND MEDALLION

Additional copies of the ribbon and "Champion" medallion are also available. Like the lapel pins, the uses of this product are only limited by your imagination. I do, however, appreciate hearing about the creative ways in which my readers have incorporated them into the reward structure of a new or existing training program. Keep the letters coming!

Any of these products may also be used to remind the others with whom you deal that they, too, can overcome whatever obstacles they meet in order to achieve their personal best. You can present a good producer with a pin or a poster to show that you appreciate his or her high performance and expect great things in the future. The pin or medallion may also be used to reward a vendor for a record of excellent service. When the pin from your own lapel is given, the reward is perceived as even more important.

Additional uses for the medallion or pin:

- Make a spontaneous gift to a good customer.
- Give a pin to your customers' or your vendors' secretaries or receptionists. Winning them over may make the difference between a good relationship with that office and one frought with difficulties.
- Use these products to reward your co-workers for helping make your job easier (for example, people from shipping and personnel as well as your own secretaries and receptionists, etc.).
- Give an associate or peer a more positive attitude by giving him or her a pin or a poster as a reminder that they, too, can be a Champion.

- Making a spontaneous gift of a medallion or pin is a great way of meeting someone whom you have been wanting to know: a local politician, head of a charitable organization, or a new prospect.
- Make certain that the person with the most friendly approach to customers is wearing a "Champion" pin.
- Reward technicians for doing the job in a timely fashion.
- Give a pin or medallion to the people in the plant who act as good team members in training and developing the others around them.
- Incorporate the pin into a system of rewards for the best salesperson of the week.
- Use the pin or medallion to reward personnel for the completion of additional training or schooling.
- Add these to the reward structure that you have already developed to thank those around you for helping you become the leader that you are.

These are techniques that have proven to work to improve the attitudes and the performance of those involved. Use them in your own life to help chip away at the obstacles that stand between you and your date with greatness.

For those of you whose advancement depends upon improving the performance of others in your organization, the medallions, pins, books and tapes may be variously combined in a comprehensive training program. My team of behavorial scientists and I are available to develop a training program to meet the specific demands of your situation. I am also available to present keynote addresses, seminars and workshops.

If any of the motivational and instructional items shown on these pages are unavailable in your area, just give us a call at 1-800-98-CHAMP (1-800-982-4267), or write Champion, 3906 DuPont Square South, Louisville, Kentucky 40207.

ADDRESSES, SEMINARS AND WORKSHOPS

In his dramatic and entertaining style, Dr. Frager leaves his audience motivated to implement the techniques that will make them — and you — champions. His outstanding presentations include the following:

THE MAKING OF A CHAMPION:
Management and Supervision Strategies

Personnel problems take up 90% of the manager's time. To be effective, managers and supervisors must learn to handle these delicate issues as well as production-related questions. Dr. Frager teaches participants proven ways to be more productive and efficient in dealing with all of the problems presented to them.

TURNING YOUR STRESS INTO STRENGTH

In this seminar attendees learn to recognize and use stress to accomplish results. They also learn to prevent the destructive stress that diminishes output. Use of these techniques will boost productivity, decrease personnel problems, raise energy levels, and reduce the risk of burnout and the associated costs of turnover.

POWERFUL PRESENTATIONS:
Public Speaking for the Terrified

Participants learn how to face any audience with the calm and confidence of a pro. They will learn to deliver powerful presentations that get results — make sales, introduce change, present reports convincingly and more.

YOUR OWN PERSONAL BEST:
"Mosquitoes Get You Every Time"

In this motivational presentation, the emphasis is on doing the little things that get huge results. Participants are exposed to techniques to improve both their professional and personal lives. Great for a kickoff meeting, after-dinner speech or keynote address.

TEAM DEVELOPMENT

A selection of exercises are available, including assessing team involvement, improving communications and increasing cooperation among team members. These seminars will strengthen your organization by showing team members that their own success depends upon the success of the team as a whole. Participants leave with an action plan for success.

THE CHAMPION WITHIN YOU:
Overcoming Adversity and Hardship

In this presentation, Dr. Frager shares his own personal fight with cancer, plus stories of others who have overcome tremendous setbacks and obstacles to become Champions. A very special presentation in which audiences laugh, cry and celebrate life together.

How to order motivational products:

You may photocopy and complete the order form in this book and send it to the address indicated. If you plan to pay by credit card, however, you may call 1-800-982-4267 with your order. Please have your credit card number ready. Your order will be shipped immediately and your questions about the available consultation services will be answered by our professional staff.

Dr. Stanley R. Frager

REFERENCES

Abramson, L. & Sackheim, H. (1977). A paradox in depression: Uncontrollability and self-blame. *Psychological Bulletin, 84*, 838-851.

Abramson, J., Seligman, M. & Teasdale, J. (1978). Learned helplessness in humans: Critique and reformulation. *Journal of Abnormal Psychology, 87*, 49-74.

Agrawal, K.G. & Dhar, U. (1983). Attribution, control, and motivation. *Journal of Psychological Resources, 27*, 21-28.

Allen, L. & Britt, D.W. (1987). Appraisal of life events, future expectations, and self-reported activity-limiting symptoms. Journal of *Educational Psychology, 15*, 132-140.

Andrews, G.R. & Debus, R.L. (1978). Persistence and the causal perception of failure: Modifying cognitive attributions. *Journal of Educational Psychology, 70*, 154-166.

Anstey, T.J. & Spence, N. (1986). Factors associated with stress in mothers of intellectually disabled children. *Australia & New Zealand Journal of Development Disabilities, 12*, 249-255.

Barthe, D. & Hammen, C. (1981). The attributional model of depression: A naturalistic extension. *Personality & Social Psychology Bulletin, 7*, 53-58.

Bebbington, P.E., Hurry, J., Tennant, C. & Der, G. (1986). Adversity and working class vulnerability to minor affective disorder. *Journal of Affective Disorders, 11*, 115-120.

Beck, A., Lester, D. & Kovacs, M. (1973). Attempted suicide by males and females. *Psychological Reports, 33*, 965-66.

Beck, A., Weissman, A., Lester, D. & Trexler, L. (1974). The measurement of pessimism: The hopelessness scale. *Journal of Consulting & Clinical Psychology, 42*, 861-865.

Beck, J. (1984). Problems encountered by the single working mother. *Ergonomics, 27*, 577-584.

Beehr, T.A. (1983). Relationship of the life experiences survey to internal/external control, social desirability, and work-related satisfaction. *Psychological Reports, 52*, 467-472.

Benoliel, J.Q. (1985). Loss and adaptation: Circumstances, contingencies and consequences. *Death Studies, 9*, 27-223.

Billings, A.G. & Moos, R.H. (1982). Work stress and the stress-buffering roles of work and family resources. *Journal of Occupational Behavior, 3*, 215-232.

Bracken, M.B. & Bernstein, M. (1980). Adaptation to and coping with disability one year after spinal cord injury: An epidemiological study. *Social Psychiatry, 15*, 33-41.

172

Brewin, C. (1984). Attributions for industrial accidents: Their relationship to rehabilitation outcome. *Journal of Social & Clinical Psychology, 2*, 156-164.

Brewin, C. (1985). Depression and causal attributions: What is their relation? *Psychological Bulletin, 98*, 297-309.

Brown, G.W., Andrews, B., Harris, T., Adler, Z. et al. (1986). Social support, self-esteem and depression. *Psychological Medicine, 16*, 813-831.

Brown, G.W. & Harris, T. (1986). Stressor, vulnerability and depression: A question of replication. *Psychological Medicine, 16*, 739-744.

Brown, J. D. & Siegel, J. .M. (1988). Attributions for negative life events and depression: The role of perceived control. *Journal of Personality & Social Psychology , 54*, 316-322.

Burns, D.D. (1980). *Feeling Good.* New York: William Morrow and Co.

Cantor, N., Norem, J.K., Niedententhal, P.M., Langston, C.A. et al. (1987). Life tasks, self-concept ideals, and cognitive strategies in a life transition. Special Issue: Integrating personality and social psychology. *Journal of Personality & Social Psychology, 53*, 1178-1191.

Cellini, J.V. & Kantorowski, L.A. (1982). Internal-external locus of control: New normative data. *Psychological Reports, 51*, 231-235.

Charner, I. & Schlossberg, N.K. (1986). Variations by theme: The life transitions of clerical workers. *Vocational Guidance Quarterly, 32*, 212-224.

Clark, L.A. & Watson, D. (1988). Mood and the mundane: Relations between daily life events and self-reported mood. *Journal of Personality & Social Psychology, 54*, 296-308.

Cohen, L.H., Burt, C.E. & Bjorek, H.P. (1987). Life stress and adjustment: Effects of life events experienced by young adolescents and their parents. *Developmental Psychology, 23*, 583-592.

Cohen, S. & Hoberman, H.M. (1983). Positive events and social supports as buffers of life change stress. *Journal of Applied Social Psychology, 13*, 99-125.

Cohen, S. & Wills, T.A. (1985). Stress, social support, and the buffering hypothesis. *Psychological Bulletin, 98*, 310-357.

Colerick, E.J. (1985). Stamina in later life. *Social Science & Medicine, 21*, 997-1006.

Compas, B.E. (1987). Stress and life events during childhood and adolescence. *Clinical Psychology Review, 7*, 275-302.

Cooper, C.L. (1984). The social-psychological precursors to cancer. *Journal of Human Stress, 10*, 4-11.

Cox, A.J. (1986). Aunt Grace can't have babies. *Journal of Religion & Health, 25*, 73-85.

Cronin-Stubbs, D. & Brophy, E.B. (1985). Burnout: Can social support save the psych. nurse? *Journal of Psychosocial Nursing & Mental Health Services, 23*, 8-13.

Crosby, G. & Clayton, S.D. (1986). The search for connections. *Journal of Social Issues, 42*, 1-9.

Csikszentmihalyi, M. & Figurski, T.J. (1982). Self-awareness and aversive experience in everyday life. *Journal of Personality, 50*, 15-28.

Degree, C.E. & Snyder, C.R. (1985). Adler's psychology (of use) today: Personal history of traumatic life events as a self-handicapping strategy. *Journal of Personality & Social Psychology, 48*, 1512-1519.

DeLongis, A., Folkman, S. & Lazarus, R.S. (1988). The impact of daily stress on health and mood: Psychological and social resources as mediators. *Journal of Personality & Social Psychology, 54*, 486-495.

Dierner, C.I. & Dweck, C.S. (1978). An analysis of learned helplessness: Continuous changes in performance, strategy, and achievement cognitions following failure. *Journal of Personality & Social Psychology, 36*,451-462.

Doherty, W. J. (1980). Divorce and believe in internal versus external control of one's life: Data from a national probability sample. *Journal of Divorce, 3*, 391-401.

Duckitt, J.H. (1983). Predictors of subjective well-being in later life: An empirical assessment of theoretical frameworks in social gerontology. *Journal of Research in the Human Sciences, 9*, 211-219.

Dunkel-Schetter, C., Folkman, S. & Lazarus, R.S. (1987). Correlates of social support receipt. *Journal of Personality & Social Psychology, 53*, 71-80.

Dweck, C.S. (1975). The role of expectations and attributions in the alleviation of learned helplessness. *Journal of Personality & Social Psychology, 31*, 674-685.

Flannery, R.B. (1984). The work ethic as moderator variable of life stress: Preliminary inquiry. *Psychological Reports, 55*, 361-362.

Fleishman, J.A. (1984). Personality characteristics and coping patterns. *Journal of Health & Social Behavior*, 25, 229-244.

Foreman, E.I., Ellis, H.D. & Beavan, D. (1983). A study of the relationship among personality traits, life events, and ascribed accident causation. *British Journal of Clinical Psychology, 22*, 223-224.

Frager, S.R. (1976). Why me? *Ostomy Quarterly, 14*, 12-14.

Frager, S.R. (1977). Why not me? *Ostomy Quarterly, 14*, 26.

Frager, S.R. (1978). If you are an ostomate because of cancer you need to read this. *Ostomy Quarterly, 15*, 43-44.

Frager, S.R. (1979). You only live once. *Ostomy Quarterly, 16*, 41.

Frager, S.R. (1986). *Stress Strategists*. Glendora, CA: Royal.

Frieze, I.H. (1976). Causal attributions and the information seeking to explain success and failure. *Journal of Research in Personality, 10*, 293-305.

Furnham, A., Hillard, A. & Brewin, C. (1985). Type A behavior pattern and attributions of responsibility. *Motivation & Emotion, 9*, 39-51.

Garfield, C.A. (1984). *Peak Performance*. New York: Warner.

Gerrard, C.K., Rezinkoff, M. & Riklan, M. (1982). Level of aspiration, life satisfaction, and locus of control in older adults. *Experimental Aging Research, 8,* 119-121.

Girdano, D. & Everly, G. (1979). *Controlling Stress & Tension: A Holistic Approach.* Englewood Cliffs, NJ: Prentice-Hall.

Goodhart, D.E. (1985). Some psychological effects associated with positive and negative thinking about stressful event outcomes: Was Pollyanna right? *Journal of Personality & Social Psychology, 48,* 216-232.

Goodloe, A., Bensahel, J. & Kelly, J. (1984). *Managing Yourself: How to Control Emotion, Stress, and Time.* New York: Frankin Watts.

Hammen, C. & Mayd, A. (1982). Depression and cognitive characteristics of stressful life-event types. *Journal of Abnormal Psychology, 91,* 165-174.

Hasse, J.E. (1987). Components of courage in chronically ill adolescents: A phenomenological study. *Advances in Nursing Science, 9,* 64-80.

Healy, J.M. & Stewart, A.J. (1984). Adaptations to life changes in adolescence. *Advances in Child Behavioral Analysis & Therapy, 3,* 39-60.

Henderson, S. (1981). Social relationships, adversity and neurosis: An analysis of prospective observations. *British Journal of Psychiatry, 138,* 391-398.

Hirsch, B. J. (1980). Natural support systems and coping with major life changes. *American Journal of Community Psychology, 8,* 159-172.

Holahan, C.J. & Moos, R.H. (1987). Personal and contextual determinants of coping strategies. *Journal of Personality & Social Psychology, 52,* 946-955.

Holahan, C.J. & Moos, R.H. (1986). Personality, coping and family resources in stress resistance: A longitudinal analysis. *Journal of Personality and Social Psychology, 51,* 389-395.

Holahan, C.J. & Moos, R.H. (1987). Risk, resistance, and psychological distress: A longitudinal analysis with adults and children. *Journal of Abnormal Psychology, 96,* 3-13.

Holahan, C.K., Holahan, C.J. & Belk, S.S. (1984). Adjustment in aging: The roles of life stress, hassles, and self-efficacy. *Health Psychology, 3,* 315-328.

Holtzclaw, L.R. (1985). The importance of self-concept for the older adult. *Journal of Religion & Aging, 1,* 23-29.

Husaini, B.A. & Von, F.A. (1985). Life events, coping responses, and depression: A longitudinal study of direct, buffering, and reciprocal effects. *Research in Community & Mental Health, 5,* 111-136.

Hutner, N.L. & Locke, S.E. (1984). Health locus of control: A potential moderator between life stress and psychopathology. *Psychotherapy & Psychosomatics, 41,* 186-194.

Hyatt, C. & Gottlieb, L. (1987). *When Smart People Fail.* New York: Penguin.

Jaffe, D.T. (1985). Self-renewal: Personal transformation following extreme trauma. *Journal of Humanistic Psychology, 25,* 99-124.

James, M. & Jongeward, D. (1971). *Born To Win.* New York: Addison-Wesley.

Janoff-Bulman, R. (1979). Characterological versus behavioral self-blame: Inquiries into depression and rape. *Journal of Personality & Social Psychology, 37*, 1798-1809.

Janoff-Bulman, R. & Wortman, C.B. (1977). Attributions of blame and coping in the "real world": Severe accident victims react to their lot. *Journal of Personality & Social Psychology, 35*, 351-363.

Johnson, J.H. & Sarason, I.G. (1978). Life stress, depression, and anxiety: Internal-external control as a moderator variable. *Journal of Psychosomatic Research, 22*, 205-208.

Johnson, J.T. (1986). The knowledge of what might have been: Affective and attributional consequences of near outcomes. *Personality & Social Psychology Bulletin, 12*, 51-62.

Kaplan, H.B., Robbins, C. & Martin, S.S. (1983). Antecedents of psychological distress in young adults: Self-rejection, deprivation of social support, and life events. *Journal of Health & Social Behavior, 24*, 230-244.

Kessler, R.C. & McLeod, J.D. (1984). Sex differences in vulnerability to undesirable life events. *American Sociological Review, 49*, 620-631.

Kobasa, S.C. (1979). Stressful life events, personality, and health: An inquiry into hardiness. *Journal of Personality & Social Psychology, 37*, 1-11.

Kobasa, S.C., Maddi, S.R. & Kahn, S. (1982). Hardiness and health: A prospective study. *Journal of Personality & Social Psychology, 42*, 168-177.

Korman, A.K., Wittig, B.U. & Lang, D. (1981). Career success and personal failure: Alienation in professionals and managers. *Academy of Management Journal, 24*, 342-360.

Krause, N. (1986). Stress and coping: Reconceptualizing the role of locus of control beliefs. *Journal of Gerontology, 41*, 617-622.

Krause, N. (1985). Stress, control beliefs, and psychological distress: The problem of response bias. *Journal of Human Stress, 11*, 11-19.

Labott, S.M. & Martin, R.B. (1987). The stress-moderating effects of weeping and humor. *Journal of Human Stress, 13*, 159-164.

LaRocco, J.M., House, J.S. & French, F.R. (1980). Social support, occupational stress, and health. *Journal of Health & Social Behavior, 21*, 202-218.

Latack, J.C. (1984). Career transitions within organizations: An exploratory study of work, nonwork, and coping strategies. *Organizational Behavior & Human Performance, 34*, 296-322.

Lefcourt, H.M., Miller, R.S., Ware, E.E. & Sherk, D. (1981). Locus of control as a modifier of the relationship between stressors and moods. *Journal of Personality & Social Psychology, 41*, 357-369.

Levin, S. (1976). The tendency to succumb to inertia. *Bulletin of the Menninger Clinic, 40*, 158-162.

Linville, P.W. (1987). Self-complexity as a cognitive buffer against stress-related illness and depression. *Journal of Personality & Social Psychology, 52*, 663-673.

Martin, M.A. & Lefcourt, H.M. (1983). Sense of humor as a moderator of the relation between stressors and moods. *Journal of Personality & Social Psychology, 45,* 1313-1324.

Marx, M., Garrity, T. & Bowers, F. (1975). The influence of recent life experience on the health of college freshmen. *Journal of Psychosomatic Research, 19,* 87-98.

McCrae, R.R. (1984). Situational determinants of coping responses: Loss, threat, and challenge. *Journal of Personality & Social Psychology, 46,* 919-928.

Menaghan, E. (1982). Measuring coping effectiveness: A panel analysis of marital problems and coping efforts. *Journal of Health & Social Behavior, 23,* 220-234.

Miller, I. & Norman, W. (1981). Effects of attributions for success on the alleviation of learned helplessness and depression. *Journal of Abnormal Psychology, 90,* 113-124.

Miller, P., Dean, C., Ingram, J.G., Kreitman, N.B. et al. (1986). The epidemiology of life events and long-term difficulties, with some reflections on the concept of independence. *British Journal of Psychiatry, 148,* 686-696.

Mitchell, R.E., Cronkite, R.C. & Moos, R.H. (1983). Stress, coping, and depression among married couples. *Journal of Abnormal Psychology, 92,* 433-448.

Mullen, B. & Suls, J. (1982). "Know thyself": Stressful life changes and the ameliorative effect of private self-consciousness. *Journal of Experimental Social Psychology, 18,* 43-55.

Murrell, S.A. & Norris, F.H. (1984). Resources, life events, and changes in positive affect and depression in older adults. *American Journal of Community Psychology, 12,* 445-464.

Mussen, P., Honzik, M.P. & Eichorn, D.H. (1982). Early adult antecedents of life satisfaction at age 70. *Journal of Gerontology, 37,* 316-322.

Newcomb, M.D., Huba, G.J. & Bentler, P.M. (1986). Desirability of various life-change events among adolescents: Effects of exposure, sex, age, and ethnicity. *Journal of Research in Personality, 20,* 207-227.

Nezu, A.M., Nezu, C.M. & Blissett, S.E. (1988). Sense of humor as a moderator of the relation between stressful events and psychological distress: A prospective analysis. *Journal of Personality & Social Psychology, 54,* 520-525.

Nideffer, R.M. (1976). *The Inner Athlete: Mind Plus Muscle for Winning.* San Diego, CA: Enhanced Performance.

Nilsen, A.P. (1983). WIT: An alternative to force. *Etc., 40,* 445-450.

Nisbett, R. & Wilson, T. (1977). Telling more than we know: Verbal reports on mental processes. *Psychological Review, 84,* 231-259.

Olinger, L.J., Kuiper, N.A. & Shaw, B.F. (1987). Dysfunctional attitudes and stressful life events: An interactive modal of depression. *Cognitive Therapy & Research, 11,* 25-40.

Ostrove, N. (1978). Expectations for success on effort-determined tasks as a function of incentive and performance feedback. *Journal of Personality & Social Psychology, 36,* 909-916.

Palys, T.S. & Little, B.R. (1983). Perceived life satisfaction and the organization of personal project systems. *Journal of Personality & Social Psychology, 44*, 1221-1230.

Parkes, K.R. (1984). Locus of control, cognitive appraisal, and coping in stressful episodes. *Journal of Personality & Social Psychology, 46*, 655-668.

Pasahow, R. (1980). The relation between an attributional dimension and learned helplessness. *Journal of Abnormal Psychology, 89*, 358-367.

Pearlin, L.I., Meaghan, E.G., Lieberman, M.A. & Mullen, J.T. (1981). The stress process. *Journal of Health & Social Behavior, 22*, 337-356.

Pearlin, L.I. & Schooler, C. (1978). The structure of coping. *Journal of Health & Social Behavior, 19*, 2-21.

Peterson, C., Schwartz, S. & Seligman, M. (1981). Self-blame and depressive symptoms. *Journal of Personality & Social Psychology, 41*, 253-259.

Peterson, C. & Seligman, M. (1984). Causal explanations as a risk factor for depression: Theory and evidence. *Psychological Review, 91*, 347-374.

Pietromonaco, P.R., Manis, J. & Frohardt-Lane, K. (1986). Psychological consequences of multiple social roles. *Psychology of Women Quarterly, 10*, 373-381.

Pittner, M. & Houston, B. (1980). Response to stress, cognitive coping strategies, and the Type A behavior pattern. *Journal of Personality & Social Psychology, 39*, 147-157.

Privette, G. (1986). From peak performance and peak experience to failure and misery. *Journal of Social Behavior & Personality, 1*, 233-243.

Procidano, M.E. & Heller, K. (1983). Measures of perceived social support from friends and from family: Three validation studies. *American Journal of Community Psychology, 11*, 1-24.

Pruyser, P.W. (1987). Maintaining hope in adversity. *Bulletin of the Menninger Clinic, 51*, 463-474.

Pyszczynski, T., Holt, K. & Greenberg, J. (1987). Depression, self-focused attention, and expectancies for positive and negative future life events for self and others. *Journal of Personality & Social Psychology, 52*, 994-1001.

Qubein, N.R. (1983). *Get The Best From Yourself.* New York: Berkley.

Rangaswami, K. (1983). Personality, life events, and alcoholism. *Indian Journal of Clinical Psychology, 10*, 179-182.

Reed, W.F. (1979). Just the prescription the doctors needed. *Sports Illustrated, 50*, 12-13.

Reed, W.F. (1986). *Born To Coach.* Louisville, KY: *The Courier-Journal* and *The Louisville Times.*

Richman, J. & Flaherty, J. (1985). The relative contribution of internal and external resources during a life cycle transition. *Journal of Nervous & Mental Disease, 173*, 590-595.

Riemer, B.S. (1975). Influence of causal beliefs on affect and expectancy. *Journal of Personality & Social Psychology, 31*, 1163-1167.

Rimon, R. & Laakso-Riikka, L. (1985). Life stress and rheumatoid arthritis: A 15-year follow-up study. *Psychotherapy & Psychosomatics, 43*, 38-43.

Rosenfeld, J.M. & Krim, A. (1983). Adversity as opportunity: Urban families who did well after a fire. *Social Casework, 64*, 561-565.

Roskin, M. (1982). Coping with life changes: A preventive social work approach. *American Journal of Community Psychology, 10*, 331-340.

Ruch, L.O., Chandler, S.M. & Harter, R.A. (1980). Life change and rape impact. *Journal of Health & Social Behavior, 21*, 248-260.

Rutter, M. (1985). Resilience in the face of adversity: Protective factors and resistance to psychiatric disorder. *British Journal of Psychiatry, 147*, 598-611.

Safranek, R. & Schill, T. (1982). Coping with stress: Does humor help. *Psychological Reports, 51*, 222.

Sarason, I.G. & Sarason, B.R. (1982). Concomitants of social support: Attitudes, personality characteristics, and life experiences. *Journal of Personality, 50*, 331-344.

Scheele, A. (1979). *Skills For Success*. New York: Ballantine.

Sedney, M.A. (1984-85). Rumination and adaptation following stressful life events. *Imagination, Cognition & Personality, 4*, 171-183.

Seligman, M. (1975). *Helplessness: On depression, development, and death*. W.H. Freeman.

Seligman, M., Abramson, L., Semmel, A. & Von Baeyer, C. (1979). Depressive attributional style. *Journal of Abnormal Psychology, 88*, 242-247.

Seligman, M., Castellon, C., Cacciola, J., Schulman, P. et al. (1988). Explanatory style change during cognitive therapy for unipolar depression. *Journal of Abnormal Psychology, 97*, 13-18.

Seligman, M. & Schulman, P. (1986). Explanatory style as a predictor of productivity and quitting among life insurance sales agents. *Journal of Personality & Social Psychology, 50*, 832-838.

Seligman, M. & Weiss, J. (1980). Coping behavior: Learned helplessness, physiological change, and learned inactivity. *Behavior Research & Therapy, 18*, 459-512.

Shadish, W.R., Hickman, D. & Arrick, M.C. (1981). Psychological problems of spinal cord injury patients: Emotional stress as a function of time and locus of control. *Journal of Consulting & Clinical Psychology, 49*, 297.

Shaw, D.S. & Emery, R.E. (1988). Chronic family adversity and school-age children's adjustment. *Journal of the American Academy of Child & Adolescent Psychiatry, 27*, 200-206.

Silberman, I. N. (1987.) Humor and health. *American Behavioral Scientist, 30*, 100-112.

Smith, T.W., Boaz, T.L. & Denny, D.R. (1984). Endorsement of irrational beliefs as a moderator of the effects of stressful life events. *Cognitive Therapy & Research, 8*, 363-370.

Stolberg, A.L. & Bush, J.P. A path analysis of factors predicting children's divorce adjustment. Special issue: Childhood vulnerability: Families and life stress: 1. *Journal of Clinical Child Psychology, 14*, 49-54.

Surtees, P.G. (1980). Social support, residual adversity, and depressive outcome. *Social Psychiatry, 15*, 71-80.

Surtees, P.G., Kiff, J. & Rennie, D. (1981). Adversity and mental health: An empirical investigation of their relationship. *Acta Psychiatrica Scandinavica, 64*, 177-192.

Tanck, R.H. & Robbins, P.R. (1979). Assertiveness, locus of control, and coping behaviors used to diminish tension. *Journal of Personality Assessment, 43*, 396-400.

Thoits, P.A. (1987). Gender and marital status differences in control and distress: Common stress versus unique stress explanations. *Journal of Health and Social Behavior, 28*, 7-22.

Thompson, S.C. (1985). Finding positive meaning in a stressful event and coping. *Basic and Applied Social Psychology, 6*, 279-295.

Trotter, R.J. (1987). Stop Blaming Yourself: Profile of Martin Seligman. *Psychology Today, 21*, 30-39.

Viederman, M. (1986). Personality change through life experience: I. A Model. *Psychiatry, 49*, 204-217.

Viney, L.L. & Westbrook, M.T. (1982). Coping with chronic illness: The mediating role of biographic and illness-related factors. *Journal of Psychosomatic Research, 26*, 595-605.

Vinokur, A. & Caplin, R. D. (1986). Cognitive and affective components of life events: Their relations and effects of well-being. *American Journal of Community Psychology, 14*, 351-370.

Waitley, D. (1985). *The Double Win.* New York: Berkley.

Waitley, D. (1980). *The Winner's Edge.* New York: Berkley.

Wells, T. (1980). *Keeping Your Cool Under Fire.* New York: McGraw-Hill.

Weiner, B. (1979) A theory of motivation for some classroom experiences. *Journal of Educational Psychology, 71*, 3-25.

Weiner, B. (1982). An attribution theory of motivation and emotion. *Series in Clinical & Community Psychology: Achievement, Stress & Anxiety*, 223-245.

Weinstein, N.D. (1980). Unrealistic optimism about future events. *Journal of Personality & Social Psychology, 39*, 806-820.

Weisman, A.D. & Worden, J.W. (1976-77). The existential plight of cancer: Significance of the first 100 days. *International Journal of Psychiatry in Medicine, 7*, 1-15.

Westbrook, M.T. & Viney, L.L. (1982). Psychological reactions to the onset of chronic illness. *Social Science & Medicine, 16*, 899-905.

Wethington, E. & Kessler, R.C. (1986). Perceived support, received support, and adjustment to stressful life events. *Journal of Health & Social Behavior, 27*, 78-89.

Whitbourne, S. K. (1986). Openness to experience, identity flexibility, and life change in adults. *Journal of Personality & Social Psychology, 50*, 163-168.

Wortman, C.B. (1976). Causal attributions and personal control. In Harvey, J.H. & Kidd, R.F. (Eds.), *New directions in attribution research: I.* Hillsdale, NJ: Lawrence Erlbaum.

Zautra, A.J. & Reich, J.W. (1983). Live events and perceptions of life quality: Developments in a two-factor approach. *American Journal of Community Psychology, 11*, 121-132.

Zautra, A.J., Young, D.M. & Guenther, R.T. (1981). Blaming — A sign of psychological tensions in the community: Findings from two surveys. *American Journal of Community Psychology, 9*, 209-224.

SPECIAL APPRECIATION

This is to everyone who has remained a friend to me through all of the rough times. These true friends were always there in moments of need, and are very precious. Like the song that my children sing, "Make new friends, but keep the old. One is silver, and the other gold." These are the people that gave me unconditional understanding and support, who helped when I was down, and expected nothing in return. Much love and many thanks!

Rose and Alfred Frager; Maris and Ed Berg; Flora and Harry Samuels; Van Vance; Wayne Perky; Terry Meiners; Lee and Sam Krupnick; Heidi Newman; Alan Aleshire; The Adult Leaders and Scouts of Troop 30 - Boy Scouts of America; The Rabbis and Staff of The Temple; Denny Crum; Jerry Jones; Mike Danneker; Peggy Danneker; Bob Blechen; Joe Eliot; Bob Escher; Bob Scherer; Barbara Zelch; Jim Glennon; Susan Berry White; Ed and Pat Lay; Barbara Domingo; Louise and Lenny Newman; Phil Yoffee; Matt Ingram; John James; The members of the Kentucky Chapter of the United Ostomy Association; Wayne Miller; Norton Waterman; Rob Levine; Milton Metz; Kathy Hammer; Rose and Jake Shainberg; Marcie and Mark Perelmuter; Emily and Steve Zeitman; Derek Smith; Daryl Griffith; Mark Reese; John Renfro; Sandy Reuben; Sherry Soll Reubenstein; Scott Goettle; Carl Bensinger; Emilie Smith; Valerie Starrett; Marty and Sandy Sundel; Lyle Sussman; Evelyn and Sid Jacobs; Jane Vance; Tom Lawson; Sam Neal; Herb Bisno; Charlie Beeler; Janet Rockafellar; Bernie Sweet; Jim Oetken; Gary, Anne, Patty and Dottie Wilson; Bill Butler; Ray Strothman; Bill Schuetze; Jackie Hayes; Guy Hempel; Bernard Trager; Amy Lawson; Margot Barr; Sidney Katz; Lin Willard; Herbert Waller; Chester Diamond; Leonard Devine; Gaylia R. Rooks; Joe Rooks Rapport; Jack Benjamin; Marianne Whyte; Seymour Slavin; Howard Borsuk; Steve Crum; Dottie Walters; Gil Eagles; Skip Essick; Mary Burns; Eileen Egan; Selma Jacobs; Margaret Tice; Anne and Gary Wilson; Joe Bowen; Sue Hughes; Joan Baptie; Randy Davidson; Professional Staff of the Old Kentucky Home Council of the Boy Scouts of America; Wayne Miller and the Staff of the American Cancer Society/Kentucky Division; Connie Sorrell and the staff of the Kentucky Cancer Program; Robin Armstrong; and all the folks at 84 WHAS.